The
SECRET
GATEWAY

More praise for
The Secret Gateway

The Secret Gateway is the kind of book I was always looking for as editor for Quest Books. It is both lofty in its treatment of the grand cosmic principles that uphold the universe and down to earth in its real-life analogies and practical applications. It can bring us closer to union with that inner self that is one with all selves.

—SHIRLEY J. NICHOLSON, author of *Ancient Wisdom— Modern Insight* and *The Seven Human Powers*

Who are we? Where are we going and how do we get there? The answers may be open-ended, but the longest journey begins with a single step. Ed Abdill opens the gate by asking the right questions and then walks with us down the road. This entertaining and highly readable introduction to Theosophy is a journey you'll want to take with him.

—ROBERT ELLWOOD, Distinguished Professor Emeritus of Religion, University of Southern California; author of *Theosophy: A Modern Expression of the Wisdom of the Ages*

The
SECRET
GATEWAY

*Modern Theosophy and
the Ancient Wisdom Tradition*

———————

EDWARD ABDILL

Quest Books
Theosophical Publishing House

Wheaton, Illinois ◆ Chennai (Madras), India

Quest Books
The Theosophical Publishing House
PO Box 270
Wheaton, IL 60189-0270

www.questbooks.net

Illustration on page 56 by W. E. Hill, originally published in *Puck*, 1915.

Cover design, book design, and typesetting by Dan Doolin.

Library of Congress Cataloging-in-Publication Data

Abdill, Edward.
The secret gateway: modern theosophy and the ancient wisdom tradition / Edward Abdill.—1st ed.
p. cm.
Includes bibliographic references and index.
ISBN-10: 0-8356-0842-5
ISBN-13: 978-0-8356-0842-8
1. Theosophy   I. Title.

BP565.A28S43 2005
299'.934—dc22   2005047543

Printed in the United States of America

To all who seek

CONTENTS

FOREWORD
by John Algeo

An old Theosophical aphorism says that Theosophy has shallow pools in which children can safely wade and ocean depths in which even giants must swim. *The Secret Gateway* is a connecting channel between the pools and the deep ocean.

In this work, Edward Abdill presents basic Theosophical concepts and ideals in simple, straightforward language. Using contemporary terms, he sets forth the essentials of an ancient wisdom and shows its relevance as a guide to practical living in the twenty-first century. He enlivens his presentation with stories that illustrate the essential points. With a minimum of technical detail, he sketches the outlines of a vast and all-encompassing philosophy of life. But, more important, he shows how to apply that philosophy in our experience of all the frustrations, challenges, and joys of day-to-day living.

Moreover, the book continually points its reader in the direction of those depths in which even the giants must swim. The author links the basic ideas of Theosophy and the simple practices of Theosophical living to some of the foundational literature of modern Theosophy. And that literature is deep indeed. So this book offers direction for those who wish to move from wading to swimming. Reading it and following the directions it offers will make the inquirer into a student and show the student how to become a true scholar of the one subject that is most important for everyone: the quest for self-discovery and self-transformation.

Preface

Ever since early childhood, I've had a powerful inner longing for the infinite. As a child, of course, I believed that the infinite was God. My mother was what I called a "lukewarm" Christian. She did not attend church, but she allowed me to go with my maternal grandmother. I went every Sunday and, when old enough, went on my own to every possible service. God was a living presence to me. Because of that, I believed what I was told about God. Sometimes on my walk home from church, the spiritual feeling was so overwhelming that I thought Jesus would appear in the clouds at any moment. Although my understanding of what God is has greatly changed, the powerful divine presence has never diminished. In fact, with deeper understanding, that presence has become more intensely real. By dropping my childish concepts about God, I have lost nothing but falsehood. What I have gained is more than words could ever express.

After graduating from high school in 1954, I took a two-year course in New York to study Spanish. One of the conversation classes consisted of only six students. The instructor of that class was a Peruvian woman who was a member of the Spanish-language branch of the Theosophical Society in New York. The city of New York had approximately eight million inhabitants, and her local

Society had no more than thirty-five members. I am convinced beyond all doubt that being in that class was no accident. It was destiny.

For a final exam in that conversation class, I chose to talk about an essay that I had written in high school. It was on comparative religion. While I was a devout Christian, I also believed that God had inspired other religions. That open-minded approach was a central theme in my essay.

The day following the exam, the instructor handed me a Spanish-language pamphlet on Theosophy. The concepts put forward in the pamphlet were quite new to me, but they sparked my interest. The last sentence in the pamphlet read, "If you doubt these things, there is a vast literature on the subject. Read and decide for yourself." That caught me. The pamphlet and all that followed from it changed my life forever.

Following graduation, I served in the United States Army for two years. On returning to New York in 1959, I joined the Theosophical Society and have been a dedicated member from that day to this. In the 1980s I was asked to become one of several national lecturers for the Society in America. Later, I was invited to branches of the Society in other countries and finally to speak at the International Headquarters in Adyar, Chennai (Madras), India. As I traveled from place to place, people often asked me to write a book. The pressure to write continued to mount, and finally a good friend and spiritual brother, Dan Doolin, e-mailed one day to say, "Why don't we have books by Ed Abdill?" That final bit of encouragement was all I needed. I hope he—and you—will be encouraged by the result.

ACKNOWLEDGMENTS

For helping to bring this book to light, the following people have my grateful thanks.

Fritz and Dora Kunz: Fritz for helping me to understand the metaphysics of Theosophy, and Dora for teaching me how to meditate.

Emily Sellon for helping to clarify so many difficult Theosophical concepts.

Joy Mills for being a living encyclopedia of Theosophical thought and history.

John Algeo for writing the foreword and for his helpful suggestions.

My friend and colleague, Dan Doolin, for prodding me to write this book.

Richard Smoley, my editor, for skillfully pointing out ways to improve *The Secret Gateway*.

Nelda Samarel for telling me the story of "The Compassionate Monkey."

My wife, Mary, whose life has made me a better person. Thanks also to her for using her computer skills to save large portions of this book from being lost forever.

And finally, H. P. Blavatsky and her teachers, without whom none of this would have been possible.

INTRODUCTION

Have you ever wondered *why*? Why is there so much sorrow and apparent injustice in the world? Why can we not find permanent happiness? Perhaps such questions have caused you to question whether or not life has any meaning. Perhaps, like most, you have decided that such questions can never be answered. Perhaps you are right—but then again, perhaps not.

Scientists have discovered that the objective world is governed by natural law. As a result, we know a great deal about matter and energy. Yet we know very little about the subjective side of our nature. Could it be that our emotions, thoughts, and spiritual nature are also governed by natural law? Current scientific method has been able to measure physical responses to emotion, but it cannot measure our hopes and dreams. It cannot measure consciousness.

There is a timeless tradition that illuminates some of the laws of the subjective nature and also addresses the question of why. It is found in human cultures all over the world from the earliest recorded history to the present. That tradition has been called by various names, such as the ancient wisdom and the perennial philosophy.

In the late nineteenth century, a remarkable woman named Helena Petrovna Blavatsky formulated a modern statement of the ancient wisdom tradition. She called it Theosophy. Blavatsky emphasized that she taught nothing new. Rather, she gathered together much of the wisdom of the past and presented it in modern language.

Here is one summation of Theosophy, adapted from a statement published in each issue of the international journal *The Theosophist*:

> Theosophy is not a religion. Rather, it is the body of truths that forms the basis of all religions, and which cannot be claimed as the exclusive possession of any. It offers a philosophy which renders life intelligible, and which demonstrates the justice and the love which guide its evolution. It puts death in its rightful place, as a recurring incident in an endless life, opening the gateway to a fuller and more radiant existence. It restores to the world the Science of the Spirit, teaching us to know the Spirit as our self and the mind and body as our servants. It illuminates the scriptures and doctrines of religions by unveiling their hidden meanings, and thus justifying them at the bar of intelligence, as they are ever justified in the eyes of intuition. You need not reject your faith in order to become a Theosophist. Rather, you are asked to probe more deeply into your own faith, especially into its mystical traditions, and to try to live an altruistic life.

The ancient wisdom tradition could never be the exclusive property of any organization. To spread its teachings, however, it was necessary to form an organization. Therefore, in 1875 Blavatsky, Henry Steel Olcott, and others formed the Theosophical Society in New York City. At its founding the Society had only one object. It was "to collect and diffuse a knowledge of the laws which govern the universe." In a very real sense, that is still the only objective of the Theosophical Society, but it is now stated as three "objects" or objectives:

- To form a nucleus of the universal brotherhood of humanity, without distinction of race, creed, sex, caste or color.

- To encourage the comparative study of religion, philosophy, and science.

- To investigate unexplained laws of nature and the powers latent in humanity.

Implementing the second and third objectives is likely to lead to the discovery of natural laws that govern our mind and feelings. Moreover, we may discover that we are all made of the same stuff and that everything we do, think, and feel will affect the whole. We may realize that we are part of a universal brotherhood, and that may change the way we live.

We already know that despite the superficial cultural and genetic differences that divide us, we are remarkably homogeneous—physically, psychologically, intellectually, and spiritually. Biologically, we are a single human gene pool, with only minor local variations. Psychologically, we respond to pleasure and pain in the same way. Intellectually, we have the same curiosity about our place in the universe and the same power to discover truth. Spiritually, we have a common origin and a common destiny.

We are part and parcel of the totality of existence stretching from earth to the farthest reaches of the cosmos in every conceivable dimension. When we realize our integral connection with all other human beings, with all other life forms, with the most distant reaches of space, we will realize that we cannot either harm or help another without harming or helping ourselves. If we know this not only intellectually, but deep within the core of our being, then our whole lives will be transformed. Responding to others with violence will become unthinkable. Our lives will become harmonious, and our lost paradise will be restored.[1]

While yet in a small minority, there are those in every culture who have realized ultimate unity. They are the saints and holy ones of humanity. They have shown us that such a realization is possible and that it leads to a life of active altruism. In time, and with a deep longing to understand our place in the world, we may become like them.

The aspiration of the true Theosophist may be summed up in the following words of Annie Besant, the second international president of the Theosophical Society:

> O hidden life, vibrant in every atom.
> O hidden light, shining in every creature.
> O hidden love, embracing all in oneness,
> May all who feel themselves as one with thee
> Know they are therefore one with every other.[2]

To the few, that aspiration is no dream but a reality. To the majority, it may be just a dream, but if so, it is a noble dream worthy of pursuit.

---

[1] The last two paragraphs are adapted from the pamphlet *Theosophy: What Is It?*, published by the Theosophical Society in America.

[2] Modified to remove gender-specific language.

The Secret Gateway has been written to show that the fundamental principles of Theosophy can be found throughout nature. Since we are part of nature, those principles also affect us. A central aim of the book is to help you discover how universal principles operate in your life. Insofar as is possible the book cites evidence from scientific and other sources to support theories expressed. Where appropriate, there are simple exercises that you may do to help deepen your experience of Theosophical insights. The book begins with a question about truth. It moves on to a presentation of Theosophical metaphysics as reasonable theory to be explored. Following that, there are chapters dealing with the inner self, the likelihood of life after death, good and evil, Blavatsky and the Theosophical Society, and a way of life that leads to freedom and bliss.

Theosophy has not solved all the mysteries of life. It has merely lifted a corner of the veil. By reading this book with an open mind and an eager intellect, you may be encouraged to probe more profoundly into your own inner self. If you do, it is almost certain that eventually you will discover that deep within your own consciousness you are one with the Eternal.

May your search be fruitful, and may it lead you to the secret gateway that opens onto a more meaningful and rewarding life.

THE COMPASSIONATE
MONKEY

Once upon a time there lived a very good monkey. He was kind and considerate of his fellow creatures. He wanted what was best for them.

One day there was a terrible flash flood, and the monkey found himself being swept away by the fierce current. He struggled to get to the shore, but he could not. He thought surely that he would soon drown.

Suddenly a branch of an overhanging tree appeared just ahead of him. He reached up, grabbed it securely, and pulled himself up to safety. The monkey was tremendously relieved. Then he looked down into the torrent and saw the fish being tossed about madly. He wanted to save them from certain death. Ever so carefully, he held the branch with one hand and reached down to save the first fish that he saw by grabbing it with the other hand. Then he gently took the fish up to safety next to him on the tree branch.

The monkey wanted to do good, but without knowing what the good was, he killed the fish that he intended to save.

To do the good, we must know what the good is.

Chapter One

THE INQUIRING MIND

As the preceding story of the compassionate monkey shows, we human beings make assumptions about what is good without always knowing what the good is. Over the centuries, widely accepted views have been codified into tenets of religious faith or presented as scientific theories, and most of us have accepted what we have been told by those who claim to know. To borrow an idea from the Rodgers and Hammerstein musical *The King and I*, we are convinced that what we really do not know is so.

Contrary to the belief systems offered by many religions, the Theosophical view is that we must discover truth within ourselves. It must result from our experience rather than from our belief.

To experience truth is to understand a principle. That understanding comes to us in a sudden, timeless flash. One minute we do not understand, and the next we do. There is no measurable time between knowing and not knowing.

When such insight illumines the mind, belief is replaced by understanding. The result of that intuitive flash is an experience of integration, wholeness, peace, and in some cases even bliss. For a timeless moment, we may say that our mind has become one with truth itself. The knower and the known have become one. There is no longer self and the truth, but only the truth. We are at one with that truth only in the flash of understanding. At the same time, that understanding has subtly changed us, even though it may take us years to fully work out the implications of the insight.

To say that truth must be experienced is not to say that intellectual knowledge is unimportant. There are many critically important facts that we must learn, such as our home address, the number of miles between our city and another that we wish to visit, or where we keep our coat. There are, however, other kinds of knowledge that we get only from experience. For example, we may read books on how to ride a bicycle, but we'll never be able actually to ride until we get on a bicycle and learn to manage it by trial and error.

What ancient sages have said or what our contemporaries teach may fascinate us. The words of others may even stimulate us to search further. Yet believing something simply because someone has told it to us is much like reading books on bicycle riding, remembering what was said, and thinking that we now know how to ride a bicycle.

H. P. Blavatsky, founder of the modern Theosophical movement, insisted that Truth could not be taught in words. In one of her key works, *The Voice of the Silence*, she writes, "The teacher can but point the way" (45). Words can do no more than that. We can express our beliefs and theories in words, but we cannot cause others to experience a truth simply by telling them.

Moreover, belief and theory alone are not only insufficient. When they crystallize into a belief system, they can actually block our understanding and spiritual development. This can be illustrated by a simple example: Some friends describe their home to us. They tell us about the various rooms, about their garden and front lawn, and even about the surrounding neighborhood. All they say is completely accurate. We form a picture of their house and its environs as they talk, and we are invited to visit. However, when we actually see the house and the neighborhood, they are different from what we had imagined. A description can only prompt us to discover the reality of the thing described. To know our friend's home, we must experience it for ourselves. When we do, it is different from what we believed, based on the description.

Likewise, if friends describe a delicious but rare tropical fruit that we have never seen or tasted, their description may be completely accurate. It is sweet, they tell us. It tastes something like a blend of mango, peach, and pineapple. Having heard their accurate description, do we now know how it tastes? Of course not. We must taste it ourselves in order to know, and when we do, it will inevitably taste different from what we imagined.

In the same way, when we hear or read a teaching or doctrine, we form an idea out of our own experience of what it refers to. But if we ourselves have not had the experience that the teaching refers to, the ideas we form about it will inevitably be false.

To say that Truth cannot be conveyed in words does not mean that we should abandon reasonable assumptions about reality. The theories may be quite accurate, the teachings sound. Yet unless we verify them both outside and inside ourselves, we will be caught in error. What we are asked to do is to realize that all theories are maps; they are not the places the maps represent.

Current scientific theories are based largely on measurement, but that method can only be applied to the sensory world. Our subjective states can only be measured in terms of their effects on the brain and body. Currently there is no way to measure our values and our beliefs, or even to prove or disprove that we have (or are) immortal souls. Yet sages from every culture and every time have claimed that there is a way to certain knowledge—knowledge of self and the universe. It is not by measurement, but by a way of life that makes us ourselves the laboratory.

Can we ever come to know the ultimate truth about the universe and our own nature, subjectively as well as objectively? We may long to discover truth, but what is truth? When Pilate asked that question, Jesus did not answer. He was silent, perhaps because ultimate truth cannot be put into words. Can we ever know who we really are? If we rely only on theory, or on the words of those we admire, we can no more know the truth of who we are than we can ride a bicycle after reading a book on the subject.

If we are sincere in our search for Truth, then we must begin with an open mind and an acknowledgment of our ignorance. We have all been conditioned by our culture and by our personal experience. It is not easy for us to rise above that in order to try to *see* accurately. Few are willing to make the personal sacrifices necessary to do that. We tend to become attached to our beliefs so strongly that we often identify with them. We *are* our beliefs. Raised in a particular culture, we say that we are Christians, Jews, or Hindus, when the fact is that we are all simply human beings conditioned differently and believing differently. We tend to ignore evidence that contradicts our beliefs, because a challenge to our worldview threatens our inner sense of security. To see "outside the box" requires courage, strong intellect, and humility. Lacking those qualities, we accept beliefs that feel comforting rather than Truth, which may require radical self-transformation. We see the emperor fully clothed when he is indeed naked. We refuse to be confused by fact.

In the following pages you will find a worldview that appeals both to reason and to the heart. Facts, theories, and subjective evidence are presented in support of this unique Theosophical paradigm. Rather than accepting or rejecting the theories, you are asked to consider the evidence and then test it out both subjectively within yourself and objectively in the outer world.

The Buddha taught that no one should accept something merely because it was written in books, ancient or modern; neither should we accept something just because he or some other sage said it. He taught that we should only accept what appeals to our own common sense and reason. That was good advice many centuries ago, and it is good advice now.

Chapter Two

_____

THE ETERNAL ONE

I n the late nineteenth century, Helena Petrovna Blavatsky
published a more modern statement of what has been
called the perennial philosophy, the ancient wisdom,
or Theosophy. What she offered was not a new doctrine
or a new belief system, but a synthesis of principles from
the wisdom tradition that has run through all the great
cultures of humanity. The subtitle of her major work, _The
Secret Doctrine,_ reads, _The Synthesis of Science, Religion, and
Philosophy_. To justify such a subtitle, she gathered evidence
from the world's religions and philosophies and, wherever
possible, from the science of her day.

The Secret Doctrine was not written to add one more
religious or scientific theory to the many already available.
It was written to stimulate both mind and heart. It was
written to inspire people to search for Truth. In spite of the
fact that _The Secret Doctrine_ appears to be a gigantic work
that might appeal only to the intellect, Blavatsky claimed
that it was written to stimulate our "higher faculties." It

was written to quicken the intuition, to lead to insight into Truth.

Everything that Blavatsky taught had one central purpose. She was convinced that the world would be an infinitely better and happier place when humanity understood its origin, place, and destiny in the universe. She believed that our behavior will change radically for the better once we understand the inner laws of our subjective nature as well as the outer laws of the physical world. In a letter to the American convention of the Theosophical Society, Blavatsky wrote:

> The ethics of Theosophy are more important than any divulgement of psychic laws and facts. The latter relate wholly to the material and evanescent part of . . . man, but the ethics sink into and take hold of the real man—the reincarnating Ego. We are outwardly creatures of but a day; within we are eternal. (*Collected Writings* 12:156)

In the proem of *The Secret Doctrine* she claims that the entire work rests upon three fundamental propositions. Here is an abridgement of her description of the first fundamental proposition:

> An Omnipresent, Eternal, Boundless, and Immutable PRINCIPLE on which all speculation is impossible, since it transcends the power of human conception and could only be dwarfed by any human expression or similitude. It is beyond the range and reach of thought—in the words of the *Mandukya Upanishad*, "unthinkable and unspeakable." (*The Secret Doctrine* 1:14)

Clearly, this first proposition can never be proven in a conventional sense. Yet there is a great deal of evidence that suggests it may be true. Modern physics, the hardest of our sciences, holds that before there was a manifested universe, there was *nothing*. That "nothing" has been called the pre-Big Bang void, eternal, boundless, nonexistent space. It is the One without a second because there is nothing to contrast it with. But it is nothing only in the sense that it is no *thing*. Both current scientific theory and Theosophical philosophy assert that out of that no-thing-ness came all that ever was, is, or could ever be. It is *that* from which all this arose. It is therefore both nothing and everything, because in that nothingness lies the potential for all, even our whole subjective nature.

This principle is "unthinkable" because we can only think by means of contrasts, and in the no-thing-ness, there is no contrast. A simple example can help bring home the truth of this idea. Imagine yourself to be alone in space. There is no air, no sun, no moon, no earth. You are completely immobile. Yet you are serene and content. Imagining yourself there without contrast of any kind, including air, can you tell whether or not you are moving through space? Do you see that without contrast of some kind it would be impossible to know if you were moving or standing still?

Consider our language, the vehicle of our thoughts. Every word we utter has meaning only because the concept it represents implies the existence of its opposite. The word *up* has meaning only because there is *down*. Similarly, the word *mountain* would have no meaning if there were no valleys or plains. *White* is meaningless without the existence of colors to act as a contrast. We can speak of *male* only because there is *female*. One could go on with nearly endless examples, but we will never find a word or concept that can have meaning without contrast. Before the Big Bang, there was no contrast. There was only an unspeakable, timeless eternity.

Perhaps humanity has always been dimly aware of that timeless eternity. In the great religious traditions of the world we find scriptures that seem to point toward this unspeakable and eternal reality. Scriptures, of course, are often better read as poetry than as prose. They are filled with metaphors woven into meaningful myths. By no means do all scriptures agree, especially if taken literally. Yet this omnipresent, eternal, boundless, immutable, and unspeakable principle of which Blavatsky speaks appears under different names in nearly all religions.

In Hinduism it is called *parabrahm*. Seeking to understand parabrahm, the student asks the teacher if parabrahm is light. The teacher replies *neti, neti:* "Not this, not that." The student probes further and asks if it is power. Again the answer is *neti, neti*. Is it darkness? Is it goodness? Is it knowledge? Is it love? To each and every question, the teacher responds, *neti, neti*. It is unspeakable.

In Judaism the sacred name of God may not be pronounced in the secular world of time. In the written word the vowel is removed, thus making "G-d" unspeakable. In the Christian scriptures we read that "No man hath seen God at any time." And in Islam, no image of God is permitted. Each of these traditions symbolically points toward the fact that this ultimate principle can never be described by words.

In every one of these religions, that unspeakable reality is said to be eternal. Moreover, the whole sensate world, including humanity, originates there. It is the ground of all being, the source of all life.

A verse of the Christian hymn "Immortal, Invisible" reveals another common thread of wisdom associated with this unspeakable reality that is called God in the West.

> To all life thou givest, to both great and small;
> In all life thou livest, the true life of all;
> We blossom and flourish, like leaves on the tree,
> Then wither and perish; but naught changeth thee.

In Genesis we read that God breathes life into human beings (Gen. 2:7). He is therefore our "true life." The dust of our bodies will wither and perish, but the inner life will not die. St. Paul speaks of "Christ in you, the hope of glory" (Col. 1:27). In John's Gospel we find: "In him was life, and the life was the light of men" (John 1:4). Then in Acts 17:28 we are told that *in* Him "we live and move and have our being." In these passages, is it not likely that the writers are referring to the divine inner life rather than to the historical Jesus? In Eastern scriptures we find a similar idea. One of the Hindu scriptures has the deity say, "Having created all of myself, yet I remain." In this view, our life is not separate from the divine life, but at one with it.

In addition to some evidence supplied by modern physics and the scriptural statements from religion, there is testimonial evidence from mystics. It is not uncommon for mystics from East and West to report a sense of unity with all that lives. That experience of unity often results in an altruistic life that is the very essence of sainthood.

Science can deduce that all arose out of the pre-Big Bang void, religion can speak of the eternal and call it God, and mystics can tell of their unitive experience with the eternal. Yet with all the evidence we have from these sources, it remains impossible for that nonmaterial reality to be *directly* perceived. Why should that be?

We have already considered the fact that without contrast, nothing would be "speakable"; that is, words are incapable of communicating meaning without the existence of something other than what the word signifies. Even "nothingness" has meaning to us only because there is "somethingness." Yet this may not be the only reason why the nonmaterial reality is "unthinkable and unspeakable."

Theosophical philosophy suggests that, however diverse our sensate experiences may be, the source of our consciousness is a point in that nonmaterial reality often called the divine self. If that is so, then we cannot *directly* perceive the source of our own being. A simple example may make that clear.

Consider the human eye. We can safely say that our eye will never see itself. We can see our eye only by reflection. One day we may be able to see every atom of our eye magnified by some instrument and projected onto a screen. Yet that image is not the eye itself. It is only its reflection.

From the Theosophical point of view, we cannot directly know the eternal, because at the very source of our being we *are* the eternal. As the medieval German mystic Meister Eckhart said, "Since we arose out of nothing, nothing is our true home."

Such an abstract idea may appear meaningless to us. What do we care about abstract space while we are so absorbed in our everyday problems? A simple meditative exercise may help us to realize how useful such a concept can be.

Since physics no longer considers matter to be hard, unbreakable stuff that occupies space, we may consider the fact that we are actually more space than substance. We, along with the rest of nature, are made up of atoms, but there is space between the nucleus and the electrons of every atom. If we could enlarge an atom so that the nucleus were the size of an orange over New York, the nearest electron would be the size of a lemon over Chicago. The distance in space between New York and Chicago takes roughly two hours to traverse by jet. The actual space between the nucleus and the nearest electron is microscopic, but in microscopic terms we can still say that there is more space in an atom than substance. It follows that we who are made up of atoms are actually more space than matter, but we seldom consider the implications of that fact.

Now let us use our creative imagination by identifying with the space of our body. We may think, "I am the space of my body." The words are used only to indicate what we are to do in the exercise. Once we understand, we may dispense with the words. Try to *be* the space. Do not imagine yourself *in* the space.

Now imagine that you, as the space, are expanding in all directions until you fill the space of the building you are in. Pause there for a few moments, or a minute, and then expand further to become the space of your city. Pause again, and then continue to become the space of the whole earth as it is gently rolled through space. Now expand to become the space of the solar system and pause there.

Now reverse the process, so that you become the space of the solar system, the earth, your city, your building, your body. At each stage it is important that you feel that you *are* the space, not that you are in it like an astronaut cut off from the space ship. The entire exercise may be done in five or ten minutes.

Many people who do this exercise report that it brings them a great sense of peace. They have identified with one of the most abstract of all concepts—space—and it has had an immediate and direct effect on them in the here and now.

Chapter Three

THE BIRTH
OF THE UNIVERSE

In some form or other, who has not asked the question posed in the Hindu scripture known as the Rig Veda: "Who verily knows and who can declare it, whence it was born and whence comes this creation?" Did a god create us? Are we an accidental conglomeration of atoms? "Who knows then," the Rig Veda goes on, "whence it first came into being? . . . Whose eye controls this world in highest heaven, he verily knows it, or perhaps he knows not" (Ballou et. al. 3–4)

Theories about how the universe came into being range from creationism to some form of evolution. The Theosophical theory of the birth of our universe begins with a simple yet profound statement by H. P. Blavatsky:

Ancient wisdom . . . attributes the birth of Kosmos and the evolution of life to the breaking asunder of primordial, manifested UNITY, into plurality, or the great illusion of form. HOMOGENEITY having transformed itself into Heterogeneity, contrasts have naturally been created. (*Collected Writings* 8:110)

According to Theosophy, the transformation from the One to the many begins with a polarization in space. Indeed, it is a polarization that is said to occur at every point in space. One pole is the objective state of the universe, or the root of *matter*. The other pole is the subjective state of the universe, or what we might call *consciousness* or *spirit*. These two attributes of reality are said to be present at every point in space and in every atom and in every creature. In *The Secret Doctrine* Blavatsky uses different terms to describe this polarization. Yet no matter what terms are used, consciousness and matter are two omnipresent attributes of reality.

There is a third attribute of reality that arises simultaneously with polarization. It is *motion*. Curiously, these three attributes—matter, consciousness, and motion—do not appear in sequence. Rather, they arise simultaneously. In other words, within the unspeakable One, there occurs a flash that transforms the unmanifested One into the manifested three-in-one. Yet these three attributes of reality are not three separate *things*. They are three, and yet still one. We have gone from the unmanifested One to the manifested three-in-one, without passing through two.

To see how this principle works, consider a bar magnet. As we all know, a bar magnet has north and south poles, and it has a magnetic field around it. Does it not seem reasonable that if we were to cut the magnet into two equal parts, one part would have only a north pole and the other only a south pole? Yet we know that is impossible. Breaking the magnet at the center produces two equal magnets, each with north and south poles, and each with a magnetic field. No matter how often we split the magnets, we always get a north pole, a south pole, and a field. These three are one.

Theoretically, our entire universe is like that, every point in it being substantive, conscious, and in motion. Would we not all agree that every atom is in constant motion? And would we not all agree that atoms are small "units" of matter? As to the second attribute, consciousness, few would believe that atoms are conscious. Yet the Theosophical theory is that indeed atoms are conscious. Certainly they are not conscious as we human beings are, but if the theory is true, they could no more be without some kind of consciousness than a magnet could be without a north pole. Moreover, they seem to "know" how to behave under certain circumstances; for example, a sodium atom "knows" how to react with a chlorine atom in certain conditions to form common salt. This may be consciousness of a kind, though not, of course, as we usually think of it.

All life has form, and therefore every living thing has a body composed of some sort of matter. When we think of matter, we think of the physical world with which we are familiar. We can detect that kind of matter through our senses, either directly or indirectly with the help of scientific instruments. Theoretically, there is more rarified matter that is not detectable with physical instruments. Although we may not be able to see it, even our emotions and thought may have a kind of substance to them. Have we not all been hit by a bolt of anger, or enveloped in a cloud of love? Perceptually, at least, it feels as though we are literally touched at some level by a force that comes from outside us.

Throughout history clairvoyants have reported "seeing" the dead. Many of them, of course, are simply deluded. Yet from the enormous numbers of reports from intelligent and sane sensitives, it would appear that at least some of those reports are true. What, then, are the clairvoyants "seeing" when they claim to see the dead? Surely it is substance of some kind. Were it "nothing," it would be not only invisible but nonexistent.

As we have seen, the possibility that matter arose out of eternal space is an idea that is compatible with religious, scientific, and Theosophical thought. By no means is there agreement on just how this manifest world appeared, but there is strong scientific evidence that matter not only arose out of space, but is a state within space itself.

One of the great twentieth-century physicists, Albert Einstein, theorized that matter is "constituted by the regions of space in which the field is extremely intense." He went on to say, "There is no place in this new physics for both the field and matter, for the field is the only reality" (Cited in Nicholson 45).

Einstein's statement is astounding. Fields are by definition nonmaterial realities. No one has ever seen a field. The only way scientists can know that a nonmaterial field is present is by the way matter behaves in its presence. For example, a magnetic field can move iron particles, but it is not by a mechanical action of physical matter that the particles are moved. It is by a nonmaterial force. Einstein is telling us that there is no such thing as matter *in* space, only an intensification of the field within space that we perceive as matter.

Further evidence that matter is not what it appears to be came in 1982 from Alain Aspect, a physicist at the University of Paris. He discovered that subatomic particles such as electrons can "communicate" with one another instantaneously no matter how far apart they may be. According to Einstein, communication through space cannot exceed the speed of light. Yet the electrons behaved exactly the same way at exactly the same time. David Bohm, a physicist at the University of London, believes that Aspect's findings suggest that electrons are not individual, independent particles. Rather, they are extensions of a fundamental reality that he calls the *implicate order*. The implicate order is a reality beyond matter as we know it. In fact, Bohm suggests that physical matter is only a ripple in the background reality beyond matter. The background reality is beyond space and time and yet, according to Henry Stapp, a physicist at the University of California at Berkeley, it affects things inside of space and time.

All this is very similar to the Theosophical doctrine that everything arises out of an eternal, nonmaterial, unspeakable reality. The reason that electrons can instantaneously "communicate" with one another over great distances may be that they and everything else are but extensions of one indivisible whole. All particles of matter, all plants, animals, and human beings are interconnected because at root they are one.

In view of Einstein's theory that matter is an intensification of the nonmaterial field, could it not be that there are emotional and mental fields as well? And could it not be that a kind of matter invisible to the eye may be the result of an intensification in those fields? If so, then our emotions and thoughts may have both a material aspect and a nonmaterial field aspect.

Just as a television set picks up signals sent through a nonmaterial field, so may our brain pick up thoughts and feelings sent through nonmaterial fields. In part at least, this may explain how the feelings and thoughts of others reach and affect us. If true, such a theory has ethical implications. What we think and feel may help or harm others.

It is said that all the matter now in our world was present at the Big Bang. That matter, however, was not then organized as we now know it. Our solar system did not spring into existence full blown immediately after the Big Bang. Even after the solar system was formed, it took unimaginable ages for plants and animals to appear, and it took even longer for the human race to emerge on earth. Who or what organized the subatomic particles into atoms, molecules, galaxies, solar systems, plants, animals, and human beings?

This brings us to the second fundamental proposition of *The Secret Doctrine,* which asserts the universal law of *periodicity*, or cycles. In part, it reads:

> This second assertion . . . is the absolute universality of that law of periodicity, of flux and reflux, ebb and flow, which physical science has observed and recorded in all departments of nature. An alternation such as that of Day and Night, Life and Death, Sleeping and Waking, is a fact so common, so perfectly universal and without exception, that it is easy to comprehend that in it we see one of the absolutely fundamental laws of the universe. (*The Secret Doctrine* 1:17)

In order to understand and fully appreciate Blavatsky's statement, we must first consider the third attribute of reality: motion. Everything that we can perceive is in motion. This was well expressed by the Greek philosopher Heraclitus, who said, "All is flux." For a more modern perspective, consider the following:

> Scientific investigations show that in infinitely little as well as infinitely great things, *all is motion* . . . we find nothing at rest. This being so, says Einstein in effect, motion must be regarded as the natural, as well as the actual condition of matter, a state of things which demands no explanation from us, for it arises out of the very constitution of the universe. It is the very essence of existence. (Cited in Nicholson 61)

Cycles of any description involve motion, and the fact that we can recognize cyclic movement reveals that the motion we observe is orderly. There are those who claim that there is no order in the universe. They are convinced that it is only our human mind that perceives what we call order. As someone once said, to suggest that there is no order in the universe is tantamount to saying that the unabridged dictionary is the result of an explosion in the printing factory. That is, to conclude that the order we see everywhere manifested around us is the result of mere random activity would be absurd. All science is based upon a search for order. If there were no order, we could have no science. It may be that order is the very nature of our universe.

Even if we accept that order is ubiquitous, we might still ask, "What or who molded matter into the forms with which we are familiar?"

Blavatsky writes that the universe and all therein is formed by "accelerated motion set into activity by the . . .

Ever to be Unknown Power" (*The Secret Doctrine* 2:551–552). Motion is therefore seen to be the creative energy of the universe.

If motion imposes order on primordial substance, then it follows that motion must somehow be orderly in itself. That may at first seem a strange idea, but if we pursue the theory further, we find some evidence that supports it.

To see how motion might be the creative power that brings about an orderly universe, consider H_2O. We all know that this substance can appear as steam, water, or ice. Although they seem to be three different things, all three are nothing more or less than H_2O. They are three states of the same substance, each state being vastly different from the other two. On a hot day we might ask for some H_2O, but we would not appreciate a blast of steam in our mouth, even though steam is just as much H_2O as water is. What is it, then, that makes these three states of H_2O different? *It is the rate of motion.* When the molecular rate of motion of H_2O is extremely rapid, it is steam. When slower, it is water, and when much slower, it is ice. In the case of H_2O, at least, we can see that motion is a creative force. The Theosophical theory is that our whole universe comes into being by the creative power of motion. Every atom, every molecule, every grain of sand, every galaxy, and all therein are but different states of one substance, just as steam, water, and ice are different states of H_2O.

Understanding that motion is both orderly and creative, we can now try to look for evidence of these qualities in the universe as we know it.

We might begin with the mineral kingdom. Crystals, for example, do not move around like cats. Yet every atom and every molecule of a crystal is in constant molecular motion. Every type of crystal has its own unique pattern of motion, and each remains itself. A quartz crystal does not become an oak tree, or even a crystal of salt. We might say that each crystal has its own destiny and that it strives only to become itself. In fact, it could do nothing else.

As we move up the evolutionary ladder, it is easier to see how motion is purposeful. Plants, for example, move down into the earth and up towards the sunlight. One reason the roots move into the earth is clearly to stabilize the plant or tree. Another is to find a supply of water necessary for survival. Lacking another source, sometimes a tree will tap into a water pipe to get the water it needs. (Unfortunately, the tree cannot foresee that such an action may cause humans to cut it down.)

The reason plants and trees lift their leaves toward the sunlight has to do with photosynthesis, by which process the plant uses the energy of the sun to manufacture food for itself. We have all observed the phenomenon with houseplants. All the leaves turn toward the source of light coming through the window. Sometimes when we notice that, we turn the plant around. What happens? In just a few days the leaves have moved around so that they again face the light.

When plants and trees move, they do not think about what they are doing. They simply follow a natural process that we might say has been developed for self-preservation and growth. Even so, motion in plants has a purpose. In the broadest sense, it is meaningful.

Animals exhibit amazing freedom of movement. Indeed, many books have been written on the significance of animal movement. Here we'll take just a few examples.

One nature documentary has an amusing segment on a certain type of long-necked birds. They are shown collapsing their necks down so that their heads are close to their body. Then they quickly stretch out their necks again to hold their heads high. This rapid accordionlike movement may look comical to us. We may have no idea what is going on, but the birds do. Ornithologists have discovered that the movement is a mating dance—funny to us, but not to the birds. The movement has a purpose, and to the birds at least, it has meaning.

When a dog is wagging its tail, we can be fairly certain that the dog is happy. When a cat waves its tail in a serpentine manner, we can be fairly certain that the cat might scratch anyone who gets too close. Consciously or not, the cat and dog are letting us know how they feel by the movement of their tails. Meaning is communicated by motion.

Human motion, both conscious and unconscious, is filled with purpose and meaning. At the unconscious level, all of our bodily organs are in nearly constant motion, carrying out their individual tasks to keep the body well. If the natural motion of our organs is disrupted by illness or drugs, the body suffers or dies.

Just as cats and dogs communicate the way they feel by moving their tails, we unconsciously communicate more than we realize by body movement. A few examples will suffice to illustrate the point.

You have decided that your ideal vacation is a camping trip to the High Sierras, but as soon as you tell your mate, you see her fold her arms across her chest. Disagreement is communicated wordlessly through motion. If you pick up the cue, you might ask if she would prefer a nice hotel near a sandy beach.

At the market, you may observe a stranger walking slowly, head down, and with a serious look on her face.

Almost without thinking, you conclude that she is sad, pensive, or depressed. The style of her walk communicates a mental-emotional state, just as surely as the movement of a dog's tail communicates a friendly disposition.

While infants cannot speak, they nonetheless do communicate how they feel. When they cry, they are responding to hunger, discomfort, or pain. But they also smile when content or happy. No one taught them to smile, yet infants do this all over the world. Their inner state of contentment or glee is revealed by the movement of muscles in the face that we call a smile. The motion of smiling is meaningful.

From the instinctual reaction of animals to the spontaneous smiles of human beings, there is a great deal of evidence that motion is meaningful. What, then, of our conscious and semiconscious motions?

One might say that every conscious motion we make has a purpose. Even the simple act of moving our hand to scratch an itch is purposeful. When we write a letter or note, we deliberately communicate through the words we write. Most of us are quite unaware of the fact that we communicate much more than that. Our state of mind and our character are somehow revealed by our script. Graphologists have accumulated a vast amount of statistical evidence that relates handwriting to character and emotional states. In fact, graphology is often used in human resources departments as one factor in the assessment of a potential employee. It has also been used in police work and has even been suggested as a means of jury selection. Graphology is not a hard science, and graphologists do not always agree on the meaning embedded in script. At the same time, the statistical evidence for some conclusions is impressive. For example, if a person consistently crosses the letter "t" with a downward stroke that appears as a gash on the paper, you can be almost certain that the person is given to rage. If it is a much shorter and lighter downward stroke, the individual may be easily irritated. Without realizing it, we express something of our subjective state by the way our hand moves over the page as we write.

Perhaps one of the most obvious kinds of meaningful motion is music. Every note of every instrument, including the human voice, is a vibration at a specific rate. It may be a vibrating string, the head of a drum, a column of air in the wind instruments, or the vocal cords of the singer. Each note vibrates outward into the air, sets the eardrum vibrating, and is perceived in our brain as a specific note. Entire compositions are only organized motion that we interpret as meaningful. It is not intellective meaning, of course, but affective meaning.

We are affected differently by different types of music. Bagpipe music, for example, has been used for centuries to stir up courage in soldiers. Lullabies are almost universally used for quieting a child. Some music tends to harmonize our mind and emotions. When music is combined with dance, it often brings the body into harmony with the psyche. No wonder that music has been used for thousands of years for spiritual and healing purposes.

Motion is unquestionably present in the whole of our physical world, but it may also be argued that motion is part of our mental and emotional world. For instance, have you ever noticed that emotions, like musical tempi, can be either "fast" or "slow"? Consider anxiety and depression. If asked to describe anxiety as either fast or slow, how would you answer? Almost without exception, people say that anxiety feels fast to them. When asked about depression, people say it feels slow.

Now consider jubilation and serenity. Would you agree that jubilation feels fast and serenity feels slow? Notice, however, that both serenity and depression feel slow, but we would far rather feel serene than depressed. Anxiety and jubilation feel fast, but we would prefer to feel jubilant rather than anxious. Clearly there is more involved than the mere "speed" of our emotions. Perhaps it has to do with rhythm or with some other factor not easily identified.

Physical motion being a fact, and emotional motion being something that we feel within us, we can now consider the possibility of mental motion. Common expressions such as the speed of thought, the quick or slow mind, and the tidal wave of human thought imply that we sense movement in the mind. In trying to solve a difficult problem, we know that we can become mentally exhausted. Our body may be energetic, and our emotions may be undisturbed, but we can't think any more. We must stop for a while. Motion, you will recall, cannot be separated from energy, and in the case of mental exhaustion the motion of our effort has tired our mind.

According to the law of inertia, matter continues in whatever state it is in (still or moving) until some outside force affects it. For all practical purposes, inertia is an everyday experience. Tailgating at 65 mph, we cannot expect to avoid hitting the car in front of us if the driver of that car suddenly slams on the brakes. Should a child throw a baseball with considerable force at a window, that ball will likely hit and break the window. If we had brakes that could stop our car on a dime at 65 mph, we would not hit the next car. If someone should catch the ball thrown by the child, the window would not break. In each case, "outside force" might be applied to overcome inertia.

Inertia in the physical world is an observable fact, but it is not only a physical fact. Inertia exists just as certainly in the subjective domain of our emotions and mind. At some point, we have all most likely had a late evening of great fun. We arrive home, as the expression goes, "all wound up," and it takes us a long time to get to sleep. Why? Is it not because of emotional inertia?

Occasionally we have all been depressed. If we do not catch it promptly, the depression grows stronger and it takes a longer time to pull out of it. The energy/motion of depression picks up momentum. Eventually either it dies out on its own or we consciously neutralize it by forcing ourselves to do something. We might take a walk, call a friend, or play some joyful music. That pulls our attention away from the depression and introduces a positive energy into the psyche, thus acting as a counterforce to overcome the inertia of depression.

Our mind, emotions, and body are all aspects of one integrated system; therefore, they affect one another. For example, if our employer is downsizing, we may be laid off. The thought of such a possibility may cause us to think about how that would drastically affect our financial state. One thought leads to another, and the sum total of such thoughts will likely create emotional anxiety. The anxiety may affect our stomach and blood pressure. Should the anxiety continue over many weeks, it could damage our physical health. Our state of mind has affected our emotions, and that has affected our body.

Conversely, if we are feeling rather bored and low in energy, we may suddenly get a creative idea about some project that has perplexed us. Immediately we feel a positive burst of emotional excitement and may even realize that we now have more physical energy. Again, an idea in the mind has affected the emotions and body.

The ancient wisdom suggests that these interconnections within us extend outside of ourselves as well. Every action, every thought, every feeling is said ultimately to affect the whole universe. Theoretically, if we drop a stone into the Pacific Ocean, eventually every atom of that vast ocean will be affected by it. Granted, we cannot see the effects of such a small disturbance, but they exist nonetheless. Similarly, every thought and every feeling also extends out beyond the borders of our own body. Modern field theory may help explain how such interconnection is possible. All matter is said to be associated with a gravitational field. Both the earth and the moon have gravitational fields. These fields are localized fields within a universal gravitational field. Even you and I have a localized gravitational field, but since we are so small compared to the sun and the moon, it is not easily detected.

Consider that our emotions and mind may be localized fields within universal fields. If that is true, then any disturbance in those fields will be communicated to the whole, just as all the bodies in our solar system affect one another through the gravitational field.

Awareness of this ultimate unity goes much further back than modern scientific field theory. The ancient Greek philosopher Plotinus wrote, "Those to whom existence comes about by chance and automatic action and is held together by material forces have drifted far from God and from the concept of unity" (Plotinus, *Enneads* 6.9.5).

The theory of ultimate unity is central to an understanding of karma. The Sanskrit term *karma* simply means "action." Theoretically, any action within the One will affect the whole, and it will cause a reaction. We know that physically every action has an equal and opposite reaction, but could it also be a mental and emotional fact?

Ever since the concept of karma became popular in the West, there has been a great deal of speculation about it. People often take a very simplistic view of karma. A common understanding of this concept is that everything we do to others will come back to us in this or in a future life. That idea is highly suspect, if not downright misleading.

Blavatsky says that karma is "the fundamental law of the universe." If that is so, and if we claim to understand how karma works, we are being either too naive or too sure of ourselves. All action in the universe, and therefore all motion, is subject to nature's laws. We may think of karma as the sum total of the laws of motion, both objective and subjective. There is a reaction for every physical action, and there is a reaction for every emotional and mental action. But while we may be able precisely to calculate physical reactions, who can say precisely what reaction will follow from our emotional or mental actions? We are beginning to learn that the psychological brutalization of children tends to produce maladjusted adults. Yet each child does not respond in exactly the same way. There are many variables. The science of psychology is in its infancy. We have not yet discovered all the laws governing the consequences of emotional and mental actions.

Have we not all sometimes been surprised at the consequences of our emotionally provoked actions? Often we make matters worse while trying to make them better, or, conversely, we are shocked by a positive response that results from our negative action. We may suddenly become quite angry with a friend and give her a tongue-lashing. Can we predict the consequences? If our friend is easily provoked to anger, she may become enraged and the friendship may end on the spot. However, if she is a compassionate and serene person, she might calm our rage with quiet, kind words and feelings. We may actually become better friends as a result. The anger, of course, will have done its damage (mostly to us), but the peaceful and loving response from our friend will have neutralized it. If we knew all the variables and understood all the laws of emotional motion, perhaps then we could accurately predict the consequences of every action. The fact is that we are not omniscient and never will be.

Many people feel victimized by their own anger as well as by other emotions. However, Theosophy teaches that we do not have to feel controlled by our feelings or spend our lives reacting to the vagaries of everyday events. We may say, "That's how I am. I can't do anything about it." But the fact is that we can do something about it; we simply do not realize it. You can discover this truth for yourself by trying the following simple experiment.

The next time you get angry, acknowledge it. Don't try to convince yourself and others that you are not angry. While boiling with rage, some people shout, "I am NOT angry." The very volume and tone of their words convey the anger that they are trying to conceal.

After acknowledging that you are angry, ask yourself, "Do I want to stay angry?" Sometimes the answer may be "Yes," because you are enjoying it. If, however, you do not want to stay angry, then take your attention away from whatever is sparking the anger and think of a tree or something in nature that has given you peace. Visualize the tree for a moment, and then try to feel its peace, its stability, and its integrity. This will not remove the irritant, but it will prevent you from adding fuel to the fire. It will also quiet your mind to some extent.

The principle of inertia operates at the emotional level as well as the physical level. How long it takes to return to a calm state will depend on how long we have been upset. If we have been simmering with anger for hours, we cannot expect that by thinking of a tree we can become completely calm in a couple of minutes. If, on the other hand, we have simply been mildly irritated, we may restore harmony to our mind and emotions in less than a minute.

When we are angry, we cannot think clearly. Often after calming down we realize what we should have said or done while we were so angry that we could not think. The mind is like a mountain lake. When the lake is disturbed by strong wind, it develops ripples that prevent it from reflecting accurately. The lake gives a distorted view of reality. So it is with the mind. Anger causes violent ripples on the waters of the mind. We cannot see clearly. After quieting the mind, we may get some insight into how best to handle the problem that sparked our anger.

We cannot leave the subject of motion without considering the nature of time. Some say that the mystery of time will be one of the last to be solved. Not only have we become slaves to our emotions, we have become slaves to chronological time. Public transportation, meetings, appointments, and even our meals are for the most part scheduled. We run our lives according to the clock, but we seldom stop to ask, "What is time?"

According to the physicists, there was literally no time before the Big Bang. That is because time is based on motion, and there was nothing to move before the Big Bang. We find the same idea in one of the first passages of *The Secret Doctrine*: "Time was not, for it lay asleep in the infinite bosom of duration" (1:27). If there is no time, then what is it that we call past, present, and future?

St. Augustine was one of the many great thinkers who have been intrigued by this question of time. He wrote:

> How can . . . the past and future be when the past no longer is and the future is not yet? As for the present, if it were always present and never moved on to become the past, it would not be time but eternity. . . . What am I measuring when I say either, by a rough computation, that one period of time is longer than another, or, with more precision, that it is twice as long? . . . While it was transient it was gaining some extent in time, by which it could be measured, but not in present time, for the present has no extent. . . . We cannot measure if it is not yet in being, or if it is no longer in being. (Cited in Fagg 119)

The way we experience time psychologically varies greatly. When we are sitting in a dentist's chair awaiting oral surgery, time seems to last forever. When we are enjoying ourselves at a party, or engaged in creative work, time flies.

One of Blavatsky's teachers calls *past, present,* and *future* "clumsy words" that are "miserable concepts of the objective phase of the Subjective Whole." He adds that they are "about as ill adapted for the purpose as an ax for fine carving" (*The Mahatma Letters* 46). Neither the past nor the future has an independent existence. There is only an eternal "now." What we call the past is the present state of all that exists plus memory. What we perceive as time is based on motion.

Motion never ceases. While any given pattern of motion has a perceivable beginning and end, motion itself has no beginning, past, future, or end. It simply *is*. Motion may be described as change or activity, and that produces the illusion of time. Yet any action, subjective or objective, does not simply vanish into an imaginary past. We and the whole world *are* the past because we are the result of all previous causes that we call the past. We create the "future" with every breath, because all action changes motion. A ripple of thought becomes a ripple of emotion, and that may bring about physical action. Change the thought before it becomes a physical action, and you have changed the "future." While the word *before* has been used, the changes and the effects are all in the "now."

Memory is a great mystery to most of us. While we have not solved that mystery, it may be that one aspect of memory is a repetitive pattern of motion within the mind. The gifted psychic Dora Kunz claimed that traumatic emotional experiences tend to leave an impression in the emotional field, or aura, that can resurface whenever we meet a similar situation. These impressions appear in the aura as swirling patterns of dense energy that she calls "scars." She says that those scars are created by repeatedly recalling traumatic events. She writes:

> To the degree that our memories are capable of giving us pain or pleasure, they are still active in us. Moreover, we seldom appreciate how often certain feelings and reactions rise up in us over and over again. If we are unhappy about something we tend to dwell

on it, and this perpetuates our involvement in the experience. Strengthened by recurring emotion, these memories tend to consolidate into symbols or scars which often look like whorls or shells, for it is their tendency to turn in upon themselves. These symbols often appear to be quite firm and solid, for they are "fed" by the emotional energy generated when we brood over an experience. (Kunz 45)

While we may not be able to see our own emotional scars, we do experience them. One of the most common is the scar of resentment. Perhaps we all feel resentful at times, but many have deep-seated resentment against a parent, an ex-spouse, or someone else. If you feel emotional pain when you think of someone you resent, Dora Kunz would say that you have an emotional scar. To rid yourself of that scar and its pain, she suggested the following simple meditation.

Take a few minutes every day to quiet yourself, perhaps by thinking of a tree, as suggested previously. Then, when you feel peaceful, think of the person you resent as being on the other side of a lake. Do not think of them as they relate to you; that is, don't think of them as your mother, father, boss, etc. Rather, think of them as just another human being. Freed from the idea that they are in some way related to you personally, send them good will. It would be foolish to try to send them love when you do not feel it. Rather, simply wish them well in their life.

Do this exercise every day for at least three months. By the end of that time you will almost certainly have reduced or even eliminated the scar of resentment. You will no longer feel pain when you think of that person. In fact, you may find that your daily meditation has affected them in a positive way. And while you may never have a close relationship with that person again, you will no longer be living in the memory of past experiences.

When we live in our memories, we are living in the nonexistent past. When we fear the future, we are also living in memory, but we are projecting that memory onto a nonexistent future. Nevertheless, memory and experience are both essential in our lives. Both memory and experience assure us that eventually we will die. Planning for old age— making a will and the like—are responsible acts. This is not living in an imaginary future. It is using common sense. The use of memory and experience to anticipate likely consequences of past and present actions enables us to live in the now and to make reasonable assumptions about what is likely to occur tomorrow. Worrying about what we imagine will happen is a debilitating waste of time. As wise people from all cultures and ages have noted in one form or another, "Sufficient unto the day is the evil thereof" (Matt. 6:34).

Chapter Four

REMEMBER
WHO YOU ARE

Before proceeding on to the third fundamental proposition of *The Secret Doctrine*, it is important to have a better sense of our complex human nature. The third proposition states that every soul is rooted in the universal "Oversoul." To make any sense of this, we must first know what is meant by the "Oversoul." Then we need to identify our own soul, or at least understand what it is that Theosophy calls the "soul." In the following three chapters we will identify the soul and the personal ego. Then we will consider what it is that survives death. In chapter seven, we will discuss the third fundamental proposition.

In Lewis Carroll's *Through the Looking Glass,* the Red Queen says to Alice, "Speak in French when you can't think of the English for a thing—turn out your toes as you walk—and remember who you are!" Most of us think we know who we are, but do we?

Perhaps we are like the man who urgently needed to get from New York to Chicago. Severe weather conditions had caused the airline to cancel his flight. An agent was trying her best to get everyone rebooked on later flights when the man rushed to the head of the line and said to the agent, "I absolutely must be on the next flight." The agent told him that he would have to wait in line like everyone else. At that the man shouted, "Do you have any idea who I am?" Calmly the agent took the mike and announced, "We have a gentleman here who seems to have lost his identity. If anyone can help him recover it, please report to Gate 36." Obviously the man thought himself to be someone quite important, and the airline agent put him in his place with a funny response. Nevertheless, she was probably right. Like most of us, he probably had lost his identity.

We may not think of ourselves as important, but many of us do think we are the physical body. Others think that they are their psychological nature, and others believe they are a soul, even though they may have no idea what a soul is. If we want to discover who we are, we must find the self that endures throughout all the changes in our body and in our personality.

Theosophically speaking, we human beings are a compound. Clearly we are physical creatures, and just as clearly, our physical nature has no permanence. Every seven years the entire skeleton is replaced by new cells. Blood, intestinal, and skin cells are also being replaced constantly. While some cells in the brain, nerves, and spinal cord may not be able to replace themselves, most of the cells in the body do. In the second half of life, thousands of irreplaceable brain cells die every day. For all practical purposes, most of the body has died once every seven years. Yet the sense of self that we feel so strongly endures throughout our whole life. If that self were only the body, surely we would be a different person every seven years, but we are not. We are still the same self.

We also have an emotional nature that is in a constant state of change. It is subject to immediate changes from moment to moment. Over the years it will undergo gradual change; for some, this change will be transformative. The self that endures through these changes cannot be the emotional nature.

We also have a mind with an extraordinary potential. Like the animals, we can use the mind to help us get what we want, but unlike the animals, we are capable of abstract thought and of self-examination. Changing thoughts run through the mind, and the way we view the world through the mind may change radically over the years, or in some cases suddenly, with a flash of insight.

Is there more to us than that? Is there anything within us that is more enduring, perhaps even eternal? To begin the search for our identity, let's return for a moment to the Theosophical theory of what many have called creation.

Religions like Judaism, Christianity, and Islam tell us that the world was created by a single extracosmic deity. Other religions and myths have similar teachings, although the deity is often quite different from the one described in the Bible. Materialists insist that there was no creator at all, but simply a coming together of matter and energy that resulted in the formation of our world and all therein. The Theosophical view is quite different. It denies both an extracosmic creator and a fortuitous concurrence of atoms that somehow came together to form the world. One of Blavatsky's teachers wrote:

Go on saying: "Our planet and man were created"—
and you will be fighting against *hard facts* for ever . . .
unable to ever grasp the whole. But once admit that
our planet and ourselves are no more *creations* than the
iceberg now before me . . . that both planet and man
are—*states* for a given time; that their present appearance—geological and anthropological—is transitory
and but a condition concomitant of that stage of
evolution at which they have arrived . . . and all will
become plain. (*The Mahatma Letters* 119–120)

The iceberg has no creator. It is a condition of water.
From the Theosophical point of view, every atom, every
galaxy, every insect, every human being, every creature visible and invisible is but a state of the one "sea." By analogy,
all are but different states of the One in the same sense
that steam, water, and ice are different states of H_2O. Theosophical philosophy is not atheistic, but it does reject
anthropomorphic concepts of the divine. Neither is its
philosophy materialistic in the common sense of that word.
Rather, Theosophy accepts multiple states of matter and
modes of consciousness, from the dense physical to the
most rarified spiritual states. These states are not created.
They arise out of the very nature of reality itself.

As we discussed earlier, when the indivisible One
polarizes, it begins the process that brings the world into
being. From an unmanifest unity, three states arise that
are fundamental to all existence. Those three states are
consciousness, matter, and motion. We think of matter as
physical stuff. However, matter at the point of polarization
is not matter as we know it. Rather, it is abstract matter, or
the potential that eventually becomes physical matter. In

Sanskrit it is called *mulaprakriti*, the root of matter. As that primordial matter evolves, it becomes seven specific states or conditions of matter, each with its own mode of consciousness and motion. As there are three states of physical matter—solids, liquids, and gases—there are said to be seven states of matter and modes of consciousness in our solar system. Six of these states are beyond the reach of our five physical senses (although not beyond our experience). In the following pages of this chapter and in the next chapter, we will examine each of these states and attempt to provide evidence for them in human experience. We refer to these seven states within us as the seven principles. Because there are no English terms for most of these principles, we must use and define the Sanskrit terms for them. We will identify four of the principles in this chapter and the remaining three in the next chapter. To merely name and define these principles would be almost useless. But to discover how they operate in us could change our lives dramatically.

If we think for a moment about the familiar physical body, it may become clear how we might benefit by discovering the deeper aspects of our nature. We know that the body needs certain nutrients, exercise, and sleep. Those who believe that they can ignore those needs will become ill and likely die an early death. We know that physically we cannot fool Mother Nature. But we are more than physical creatures. We have emotions, a mind, and more profound states within us. Those states, or principles, are also part of nature. By discovering those inner principles and understanding how they operate, we can learn how to live a healthy and joyous interior life. Moreover, we may discover that some of those principles are part of the immortal, reincarnating self. We will begin with the inner-most principles, those that are said to be immortal.

The first principle is known by the Sanskrit term *atma*. It may be defined as a point in unconditioned consciousness, or consciousness without an object.

We almost always think of consciousness along with its objects. We are conscious of our environment, of the people we see, the sounds we hear, the feelings and thoughts that we are experiencing. Atma is said to be a point in pure, unconditioned consciousness itself. It is consciousness alone, not what consciousness perceives. More accurately stated, atma is a point in the ultimate real, or what Blavatsky called "Be-ness."

Have we not all occasionally awakened in the morning or after a nap and for a split second simply had a sense of "am"? In that brief flash there is not even a sense of self. There are no objects of consciousness. There are no thoughts. There is only what Blavatsky called "Be-ness." Almost immediately the objects of consciousness come into the mind. Where am I? What day is this? What are my plans for today? Before all that, there is just "Be-ness." It is consciousness itself without any object. In that momentary flash we simply *are*.

The moment the mind brings in the objects of consciousness, the emotions respond. We realize that it is Monday and we have to go to work. Or we might remember that we have a dental appointment, or a pleasant day planned with friends. Whatever the object of consciousness, our emotions respond. The dental appointment may make us anxious, while the prospect of a pleasant day may bring a happy feeling. The awareness itself does neither. It is beyond pleasure and pain. It simply *is*. It is when we identify with the objects of consciousness, with the "me" and all its plans, problems, and pleasures, that our state of mind is profoundly affected.

Having considered consciousness without an object, we may now turn to the theory that we are ultimately a point in consciousness. Strictly speaking, a point has absolutely no dimensions at all. It is a mathematical concept whose one property is *locus*, location. A dot may represent a point, but every dot, even if it is only one atom thick, is made of substance and is therefore three-dimensional.

If we are one-pointed in consciousness, we cannot *consciously* attend to more than one thing at a time. Surely everyone has had the experience of talking on the phone when someone in the room begins to talk to us. For a while, we try to listen to both, but eventually we realize the futility of it and ask the person on the other end of the line to hold on while we listen to the person in the room. We can *hear* both simultaneously, but it is impossible to *listen* to both at the same time. We are one-pointed in consciousness, even though the sound of both voices reaches the ear and brain.

Although we can do several things at one time, we can give our *conscious* attention to only one thing at a time. For example, we can rub our stomach and pat our head at the same time. While doing that, we can carry on a conversation. Before we are able to do these things simultaneously, however, we had to learn to rub our stomach and pat our head at the same time. At first we were likely to pat both the head and the stomach or rub both. Eventually we solved the problem by paying attention to only one hand. Once we had one hand patting our head, we put our conscious attention on rubbing our stomach with the other hand. After the task had been learned, we were able to put our conscious attention on holding a conversation while the subconscious took care of the rubbing and patting exercise.

For further evidence that we are one-pointed in consciousness, you might take a moment to try the following simple experiment.

Close your eyes and imagine yourself on two sides of a street at the same time. Do it any way you choose, but be sure that there are two of you. Do not imagine that you are simply expanding to cover the street. That would be only one of you.

Having done that, ask yourself, "Where was I when I observed those two images of myself?" Some of you will answer that you were above the street looking down on two people, both of whom were you. Others will have stood on one side of the street and observed themselves on the other side of the street. Still others will have stood in the middle of the street and observed themselves further down on both sides of the street.

Notice that however you did it, you were looking at two images of your self from a third point. You were really only in one place at a time, however many images of your self you might see.

Theosophically speaking, you are the eternal self—a point in unconditioned consciousness. The body, emotions, and mind and all other aspects of our nature will change. All the objects of our consciousness, and all the experiences with which we tend to identify, will pass away. Only the immortal self can never change because it is uncompounded. It is a point in eternity.

The second principle is called *buddhi*. St. Paul spoke of a threefold nature in humans. He called them spirit, soul, and body. From the Theosophical point of view, atma, along with buddhi, is the spirit. They are both impersonal aspects of our nature. Atma is a point in the eternal. As such, it has no individual aspects such as we find in the personality. Buddhi may be described in several ways. It is the first sheath over atma. It is universal mind, cosmic ideation, wisdom, and bliss, and from it comes what we call spiritual intuition or insight. At first glance, these descriptive words seem incongruous. How could universal mind possibly have any connection to bliss? Despite the apparent incompatibility of terms, they are interconnected, and we can and do experience buddhi in our lives.

At times we all make an intense mental effort to understand a principle. It may be a mathematical one, an artistic one, or even a mechanical one; that is, how does something work? At first the unifying principle eludes us. Then, when we relax the mind for a moment, the understanding comes in a flash. There is no measurable time between not knowing and knowing. We exclaim, "Aha! I get it." Simultaneously, we feel elated, happy, and we smile. We experience a touch of bliss.

The "aha" experience does not come gradually. We never hear anyone exclaim, "Aaaaaaaaaa-ha!" It is always a sudden "aha!" We have had an insight, a kind of spiritual intuition that has flashed on our mind from the level of what may be called universal mind, or buddhi. It is a truth that is totally impersonal. It is an insight into a truth rather than some individual piece of information. The principle is universal. It is always true, whether or not we have some object that reveals the principle. It is also always true whether or not we get it. Some will, some won't. The principle remains the same, just as the principle of gravity has always been true even before humans were aware of it.

In common speech, the word *intuition* usually refers to what we might call a psychic hunch. Many of us have at one time or another had a vague, or even specific, sense of the state of mind of a friend who is miles away from us. We seem to know that they are thinking of us, or that they are extremely upset. Later we discover that without our having been informed of their state, this psychic hunch turns out to have been right. More commonly, we sometimes think of someone just before they call us on the phone. We may even be tempted to answer by saying, "Hi, Jack." This is one common example of a psychic hunch.

The July 2004 issue of the *Journal of the Society for Psychical Research* has an article by Rupert Sheldrake, Hugo Godwin, and Simon Rockell entitled, "Filmed Experiment on Telephone Telepathy with the Nolan Sisters" (18–72) that gives statistical evidence for the reality of this typical form of psychic occurrence. In the experiment a participant was told that at a specific time he or she would receive a call. The call would come from one of four friends. The friend who was to make the call would be chosen at random by throwing a die. As soon as the phone rang, the participant was asked to say who was calling before picking up the phone. Getting the name of the caller right by chance would mean that about 25 percent of the time the receiver would be right. In fact, in more than 850 trials with 65 participants, the success rate was 42 percent, a statistically significant percentage. There are of course many other examples of the phenomenon, some of which are quite dramatic.

The psychic hunch is quite common; often it is remarkably accurate. It is what we usually mean by the term *intuition*. When we describe buddhi as spiritual intuition, however, we are not speaking of a psychic phenomenon. We are speaking of direct insight into a truth.

The word *intuition* has in recent years been used by some of our greatest scientists. Einstein said that intellect has little to do with discovery. He claimed that at the moment of discovery there is a "leap in consciousness" that we might call intuition. When that happens, one gets the solution without knowing how or why (cited by Nicholson 165–66).

Brian Josephson, a physicist and Nobel laureate, has also acknowledged the role of intuition in discovery. He said, "It's much more a matter of getting the intuition of how things are and then thinking through to see whether the intuition fits the facts" (Nicholson 166).

We may not be research scientists, but we all get flashes of insight from time to time. Factual perception is not insight. Should we witness a traffic accident, we can see what has happened. We know which car hit the other, and we may be able to determine which one caused the accident. Although we may know certain laws of physics, such as the simple fact that two physical objects cannot occupy the same place at the same time, we do not get a flash of insight that produces bliss. In fact, quite the opposite is true. We are horrified by the event.

On the other hand, if we are searching for *meaning* and *purpose* behind and within perceived facts, then we may suddenly get a flash of understanding into a universal principle. It does not matter whether we are trying to understand what is behind a computer problem or a spiritual problem. When we "get it," we get the principle behind that situation and any similar situation at any place and time. As opposed to a perception of facts, we have experienced a flash of timeless truth from buddhi. The perceived facts may be accurate, but their perception does not produce bliss. The understanding of universal principles always brings bliss.

To further test out this theory, look at the optical illusion printed below. There are two distinct images within the picture. Once you have seen one of them, try to discover the other one. Whether or not you have seen this image before, try again to see one image, and then discover or rediscover the second one. If you have difficulty seeing the second image, keep trying until you do. At the moment you discover the second image, how do you feel? Almost

everyone responds with a big smile and an "Oh, I see it now." There is a very distinct difference in "meaning" between the two images. Everyone sees the black-and-white lines, but only when those lines come together in the mind as a meaningful whole do we get a flash of understanding and a moment of bliss.

Now you might try one more experiment. Try to see both images at the same time. You now know that the nose of the old lady is the chin of the young lady, but in focusing on the young lady can you actually *see* the old lady at the same time? This will almost certainly be impossible. We can know that the other image is there, and we can even know which lines would reveal it to us if we refocused, but we cannot experience the two images in the same way at the same time.

This experiment may further convince us that our human consciousness is one-pointed. If it were otherwise, we would have no difficulty focusing on more than one thing at the same time.

Such an experiment does not deny that we have peripheral vision. We might focus on a tree in our yard and simultaneously be aware of its surroundings. However, you will likely find that you cannot focus on both the foreground of the tree and the background of its environment at the same time. A shift of focus is required in order to see the other clearly.

Atma-buddhi, considered together as one, is what we call the Spirit. It is indivisible and it is universal. Theoretically, it is the very root of consciousness and the source of life. In it "we live and move and have our being." While it is impersonal, we may experience it as the one true, immortal self. In *The Voice of the Silence* we read:

That which in thee *knows*, for it is knowledge, is not
of fleeing life. It is the man that was, that is, and will
be, for whom the hour shall never strike. (31)

This statement may seem strange, even impossible. Yet
if you reflect back to any moment when you got a flash of
understanding, you may realize that when that instanta-
neous understanding occurred, there was only the knowledge itself. That is, in that timeless flash, you were not
aware of both "me" *and* the knowledge. There was only the
knowledge. The knower and the known became one. Almost
immediately, of course, we revert to identification with the
"me," and there is once again apparent duality, the "me"
and the knowledge.

By now it should be easy to see that the knowledge
itself is impersonal. It is not my truth as opposed to your
truth, for there is only truth itself. It does not change from
person to person. Granted, we often get but a fragment of
truth, and each may get different fragments. However, if
the fragment that we get is true, it does not change from
person to person.

When the knower and the known become one, who
is the knower? Clearly, the knower is individual. Were
that not so, everyone would have the same insight at the
same time. This brings us to the third principle, called
manas. The Sanskrit term *manas* has often been translated
as "the one who knows," or "mind." To most of us, mind
is associated with academic ability and logical thinking. It
is that, but it is more than that. Manas is that within
us which grasps not only logical thinking, but artistic
ability, empathy, and talents of all kinds. It is the mind
(manas) that understands truth. It is the mind that can

distinguish right from wrong, and it is the mind that gives rise to our character.

Blavatsky's *The Voice of the Silence* says, "The mind is the great slayer of the real. Let the disciple slay the slayer" (1). That may be the most misunderstood statement in Theosophical literature. Surely we are not to become idiots. If we had no minds, we would be less than animals. The writer of *The Voice of the Silence* said that Theosophy was for those who can think. Therefore, when she asks us to "slay the slayer," she could not possibly have meant that we should become mindless. What, then, might her meaning be?

An important clue to solving the apparent contradiction is the fact that mind has two major functions. In Theosophical literature these functions have sometimes been called "higher mind" and "lower mind." Unfortunately, the terms "higher" and "lower" tend to cause many to think that the higher mind is better than the lower mind. One is no better than the other any more than one kidney is better than the other. They are two distinct functions of one mind.

Rather than using the terms "higher mind" and "lower mind," let us use the Sanskrit words *buddhi-manas* and *kama-manas*. By so doing we avoid the common value judgment associated with higher and lower.

When the mind is open to the abstract, when it understands, when it is flooded with an insight, it is called buddhi-manas because it reflects buddhi. This may become clear if you consider that all of our concepts are abstractions. Along with many animals, we perceive the objects around us. A cat can see a chair, a table, and a computer. It knows that in most cases it can leap onto those objects.

However, there is no evidence whatsoever that a cat groups chairs of every description into a concept that we might call "chairness." It is the same for colors. We and many animals can distinguish blue from yellow. We humans can see many different shades of blue, and we group them into the concept of "blueness." However, no one can *see* blueness. It is an abstraction.

Likewise, we can entertain the concept of infinity, or the pre-Big Bang void. No one can see that, nor is anyone likely ever to see it. Yet our mind accepts the existence of infinity as not only reasonable but very likely true. No animal has ever given evidence that it can grasp such an abstraction. With the possible exception of some of the higher anthropoids, animals appear to lack the conceptual ability that we associate with buddhi-manas.

The higher mind, or buddhi-manas, is our true individuality. It is the reincarnating ego, the self that endures through all our incarnations.

The mind has sometimes been depicted metaphorically in legends and scriptures as a thief. In the New Testament we read that Christ was crucified between two thieves. One of the thieves recognizes Christ, and the Lord tells him that he will be with him in paradise that very day. The other thief does not recognize Christ, but only perceives another man who is dying. Jesus does not tell the second thief that he will be with him in paradise. Whether or not the crucifixion story is historical fact, the thieves may represent the two functions of mind. Buddhi may be seen as the Christ principle within each one of us. The New Testament credits Jesus with saying, "The kingdom of God is within you" (Luke 17:21), and St. Paul speaks of "Christ in you, the hope of glory" (Col. 1:27). Could it not be that both Jesus and St. Paul were referring to the eternal and divine principle within?

When the individual mind reflects that inner, universal principle called buddhi, or the Christ principle, it is called buddhi-manas. Only this aspect of the mind can be with the divine in paradise.

The other thief may represent what has been called the lower mind, or kama-manas. This function of mind deals with percepts (that is, objects of perception), and it is associated with emotion.

As soon as we turn our attention toward the objects of perception, we awaken emotion. We awaken *kama*, our fourth principle. Kama may be thought of as our craving nature, our emotional nature, our feelings. Animals as well as humans exhibit this principle. While we can distinguish between a thought and a feeling, both are linked together like two sides of a single coin. If you think about it, you will probably realize that every concrete thought is associated with some feeling, however dim it might be. Conversely, every feeling is associated with a thought, however vague it might be. We can all distinguish a thought from a feeling, but can we ever completely separate the two? Do not thought and feeling always come together? Any thought associated with a percept is coupled with some kind of emotion. The object may be physical, or it may be an "object" in our mind. It is not that every percept brings strong emotion, but it usually has some emotional content accompanying it. We *like* some chairs more than others. If we can afford it, we buy furniture that pleases us most. Think of any object of perception, and you will likely discover that it engenders some emotional reaction, however minimal.

You might remember a time when you felt anxious but had no conscious thoughts that were associated with the feeling. Yet almost certainly there was a thought in your subconscious that produced that feeling. It may take hours, or even years, before you discover it, but you can be almost certain that the thought and the feeling are linked together.

Since kama is always associated with mind, we use the term *kama-manas* when referring to our thinking, feeling nature. A prominent Theosophist describes this connection between mind and emotion as "flinking," a combination of "feeling" and "thinking."

What has been called the "associative principle" is an aspect of kama-manas. It is the ability to associate one thing with another, even when they are unrelated. Both animals and humans have this ability. Were it not so, animals could not be trained to do tricks. The famous experiment of the Russian behavioral psychologist Ivan Pavlov illustrates this principle perfectly. As most people know, Pavlov repeatedly rang a bell that a dog could hear, and then he fed the dog. He did it so frequently that the dog began to associate the bell with food, and, on hearing the bell, the dog would salivate in anticipation of being fed. Then he rang the bell without feeding the dog. Nevertheless, the dog salivated. The dog had learned to associate the bell with food.

The advertising industry relies heavily upon the associative principle in kama-manas. Advertisers try to link their product with prestige, sex appeal, gaining respect, and so forth. Many years ago, a bank put on a television commercial advertising a certificate of deposit. A substantial minimum of cash was required to obtain the advertised certificate, so the commercial began with a man seated at a desk in his study. He was obviously well off. In the background one could hear a grandfather clock going "tick-tock, tick-tock, tick-tock." The gentleman began to write out a check to the bank, while the announcer was telling of all the wonderful financial benefits that would come to those who purchased a certificate of deposit. At the close of the commercial, the man blotted his check and the announcer said, "So think about it." Then all was quiet except for the grandfather clock that continued to go "tick-tock, tick-tock, tick-tock." Obviously, the sponsor was appealing to an affluent audience that was likely to have grandfather clocks. The hope was that the next time potential patrons heard the ticking of the grandfather clock, they would immediately think of a certificate of deposit and write out a check to their bank to buy one. Just as Pavlov tried to condition his dogs, the advertiser tried to condition us.

In idle moments we experience what has been called a stream of consciousness. One thought occurs to us, and that leads us to another one, and that to yet another, and so on. It might be helpful to observe this process in your own mind. If you do that, you will likely discover that your mind is attracting your attention to a series of images, or memories, of past events. Your mind is running on automatic without any direction from you. The first step in gaining mastery over the mind is to recognize that fact. If we do, then we may use the associative principle to good advantage. Professors, writers, and stand-up comedians all make good use of the associative principle. Whatever our line of work, we can, too. At the same time, it is important to understand that the associative principle is one of the factors that allows our mind to become conditioned.

It is only the aspect of mind known as kama-manas that can be conditioned. Buddhi-manas is beyond psychological conditioning. It is our divine nature. For this reason, buddhi-manas is called the spiritual soul, and kama-manas is called the animal soul. The former endures throughout many incarnations, while the latter gradually disintegrates after physical death. The human soul is manas itself. When it is associated with buddhi, it is spiritual. When it associates with kama, it is animal. Using our free will, we may associate with either.

It is important to understand that while there are two distinct functions of mind, there is only one mind. Reflected in buddhi, it is called buddhi-manas. Reflected in kama, it is called kama-manas. Whether reflected in the one or the other, it is still the same manas.

Our sense of "me" is formed at the juncture of kama-manas and buddhi-manas. A moment's thought may make that clear. When the mind is open to the abstract, there is no sense of the personal self. However, as soon as the mind focuses on the objects of perception, there is a strong sense of "I" and "not I." The observer perceives the observed and realizes the difference.

Chapter Five

THE EGO, THE PERSONALITY, AND THE BODY

M any years ago, Hughes Mearns wrote a humorous verse that goes:

> As I was going up the stair
> I met a man who wasn't there.
> He wasn't there again today.
> I wish, I wish he'd stay away.

The man on the stair is the personal ego. He is both there and not there. He is a powerful illusion. But what is that illusion, and why are we so convinced that it is the self?

When we are born, we are helpless infants. At the beginning of our lives, we do not even have a sense of where our physical body begins and where it ends. An infant will wave its arms in the air, put a finger in its mouth, and bite. Were the child able to speak, it might exclaim, "Wow, that moving thing in the air is part of me!" Eventually, of course, the child realizes the limits of its own physical body. That body is "me."

No matter the culture into which the child has been born, the gender of the child is quickly identified. If the child is a girl, she tends to be treated in conformity with the cultural norms of her birthplace. If a boy, he too is treated as his culture dictates. Eventually the child realizes that there are girls and boys and learns its own gender.

Ever so slowly we begin to form our self-image. "I am a girl" or "I am a boy" is just the beginning. The way we are treated by our parents and those around us greatly influences this growing self-image. Our parents may love us and treat us well, or they may consider us to be an unwanted burden and treat us poorly. Let us consider two extreme cases.

Many children are born in terrible neighborhoods. They may have a mother who does not love them and a father who is seldom or never around. As growing children, they have felt rejected and worthless. They have been told that they are no good, and they have been treated that way. In such a case, the child is likely to develop a negative self-image. The child thinks, "I am no good." Such an attitude becomes embedded in the subconscious. If circumstances do not change throughout childhood, it is extremely difficult to alter that self-image. At age fifty, we may still think we are no good. Perhaps we become violent, hating humanity because some humans gave us a raw deal. Or we might become reclusive, believing ourselves unwanted. We may think, "The world is a bad place. People are bad. I am bad." The way we react to a negative self-image varies, but its damaging effects will persist in life unless we recognize the problem and overcome it.

Of course, the opposite may happen as well. Many children are born into loving, caring families. If the parents love their child, are always there for the child, and encourage the child to develop his or her potential, then the child is likely to form a positive self-image. The result may be a person who makes friends easily, believing, "The world is a good place. People are good. I am good." Unfortunately, when parents are convinced that their child can do no wrong, the child may grow up ready to give God daily advice. Such a child may become an intolerable egotist. Whatever self-image we may hold, it will continue to affect us so long as we hold that image to be the self.

Very likely, the way we habitually react to personal experience affects our self-image more profoundly than anything else. Many people think of themselves as shy. Have you ever thought of how that self-image may have been developed? It could well be that when you were in first grade, the teacher asked you to tell the children about your summer vacation. You had a wonderful vacation, and you were eager to share your experience with everyone. As you were enthusiastically telling your story, suddenly the entire class, including the teacher, burst into uncontrolled laughter. You had no idea what you said or did, but everyone was laughing at you. Imagine how you would feel. Imagine what reaction you might have had to that experience. In many cases, the child makes an unconscious resolve never to do that again. The child thinks, "I will not expose myself to ridicule. To avoid it, I will never speak in public again."

While this case is exaggerated to make the point, the fact is that people who have had an experience like that may think of themselves as shy, even when they are seventy-five years old. Had their experience been different, they may not have become shy at all. Their reaction to that negative experience convinced them to keep quiet. Long after the event, they believe they are unable to speak in public because they are shy.

When some event causes us to respond with strong emotion, the way we respond tends to become embedded in the subconscious. Thereafter, every time a similar event occurs, the associative principle of the mind kicks in. Unconsciously, we "see" the previous event and we have a knee-jerk reaction. We respond to the new but similar situation just as we did the first time. We repeat the initial response, and by so doing, we strengthen the emotional pattern in the subconscious. Furthermore, we begin to think of that pattern as an inherent aspect of "me." We say, "I can't help it." Yet, since it is no more than a psychological pattern that we have created, we can neutralize it without harm to the true self.

The psyche is filled with emotional patterns. None of them, singly or collectively, is the true self. Consciously or unconsciously, we have created every pattern, and we can neutralize every pattern. Yet the sum total of those thinking-feeling patterns becomes the "me" that we believe we are. In psychological terms, we have identified with the conditioned mind. When we identify with that, it becomes the personal ego. Like the man on the stair in the poem, that ego is both there and not there. It appears real to us when we identify with it, but it vanishes when we realize that the personal ego is an illusion caused by our identification with temporal emotional-mental patterns. The patterns exist, but when we think they are self, we are deluded.

Up to this point, we have considered four of the seven principles. Atma and buddhi together are the spirit. Manas, when it reflects buddhi, is the spiritual soul, or the reincarnating self. Manas, when it is associated with kama, is what has been called the animal soul. The latter is transient, perishing between incarnations, while the former is immortal. Whether associated with buddhi or kama, manas is the human soul. The personal ego is an illusion with which we tend to identify. It is formed by the thinking-feeling patterns in kama-manas.

Unconsciously, we identify with our feelings and thoughts. We say, "I am happy or unhappy." But who is that "I?" *The Voice of the Silence* tells us that we must give up self to non-self. That is, we must destroy the illusion that our conditioned mental and emotional states (the personal ego) are the true self.

The fact that all human beings develop a personal ego should be evidence enough that the ego plays an important part in human development. While we are centered in kama-manas, we are motivated from that point. Desire (kama) prods us to act, our actions bring consequences, and we learn from these consequences. This is a vital stage in our evolution. An analogy may help make this clear.

The ego is like the shell of a chicken egg. When the egg is laid, it is important that it have a firm shell to isolate it from its environment. If there were no shell, or if the shell were to be broken prematurely, there could be no chicken. As the chick develops, however, there will come a time when the shell blocks further growth. The chick must destroy the shell from within or the chick will die. In the analogy, the shell of our ego serves to assure natural development. When the inner self begins to awaken within the ego shell, it must break that shell. Like the chick, we peck at it bit by bit until at last it is broken and we are born free.

It is important to distinguish between the *personal ego* and the *personality*. After the ego plays its part in our development, we must destroy it. But in so doing, we do not destroy the personality. The personality is our *modus operandi*. It is our unique way of functioning; it is our temperament. Among other things, the personality consists of our talents and personal preferences, such as the kind of entertainment we enjoy, or whether we tend to be gregarious or not. It is neither the ego nor the inner self. It is what we might call the *personal* self, the temporary vehicle of the inner self. The personality is transient in the sense that it dies after each incarnation. It cannot be killed before the death of the body. If it were possible to kill it, we would be left with a physical body incapable of expressing anything more than physical needs.

Having distinguished between the ego and the personality, we may now consider the three remaining principles that are part of our human nature: *linga sharira, prana,* and the physical body.

Have you ever wondered how our body is formed, and what holds it together during life? Blavatsky claims that it is what we might call a dynamic force field. She called it by the Sanskrit term *linga sharira,* but we can use one of two English terms: the *etheric double* or the *vital body*. The claim is that the etheric double is formed before the physical body. Unlike the static field around a bar magnet, this field is dynamic and ever-changing. The field is said to hold the physical cells together just as the magnetic field of a bar magnet holds iron filings by its force. The Sanskrit word *linga* may be translated as "model" or "pattern"; hence it is the form (or field) that is the pattern for the physical body. In a sense, the etheric double is the result of our physical karma. Some of us are born whole and healthy, others with a weak heart or a missing kidney. The physical condition is an exact duplicate, or double, of the field. It is the field, the etheric double, that molds the growing fetus and the growing child and adult.

While science has not yet proven that such a field exists, there is some remarkable evidence that supports this theory. Most of us think of the heart as a pump. The heart pumps blood through the body. That seems reasonable enough, but if it is the physical heart that does the pumping, then we must have the heart before any pumping begins. Surely there could be no pumping before we have the pump. That, however, is not the case in a chicken egg. As the chick begins to develop within its shell, there appears a pulsation in the place where the heart will be formed. There is as yet no heart, only a pulsation, a pumping. Is it not possible that the dynamic force field known as the etheric double is causing the pulsation? Just as iron filings respond to the presence of a magnetic field, protoplasm may respond to the presence of the etheric double, or what we might call a psychodynamic field.

Yet another piece of striking evidence suggests the presence of the etheric double as a field. In the early 1950s a biologist by the name of William Seifriz, of the University of Pennsylvania, set up an experiment with slime mold. Slime mold is a primitive form of protoplasm. It streams in one direction and then in the opposite direction in a regular pattern taking a few seconds. Seifriz timed the movement of the slime mold that he planned to use in his experiment. When he had the time accurately noted, he anesthetized the slime mold. The movement came to a halt. When the anesthesia wore off, he expected what most of us would expect. He thought that the slime mold would continue moving from where it had stopped. Say it would take the slime mold six seconds to stream from right to left and six seconds to stream back from left to right. Now suppose that the anesthesia arrested the flow at four seconds into its streaming to the left. When the anesthesia wore off, one would expect that the slime mold would continue to stream to the left, thus completing its cycle. However, the slime mold did not do that. Instead, it began to stream to the right. Since the experiment had been timed, Seifriz was able to determine that if he had not anesthetized the slime mold, it would have been streaming to the right at the exact moment that the anesthesia wore off.

To understand how this might have occurred, we need only sprinkle iron filings on a piece of paper and hold a bar magnet under the paper. Now move the magnet back and forth at a timed rate. Obviously the iron filings will sway back and forth in response to the moving field. Next we keep the paper and the filings where they are, but we move the magnet down so that the paper and filings are outside the reach of the field. At the same time, we continue to move the magnet back and forth at the timed rate. The field continues to move, but the iron filings are still. If we continue moving the magnet while raising it toward the paper, eventually the field will once again affect the filings, and they will move in response to the moving field.

In this experiment, we can see that the iron filings are the test object for the magnetic field. In the Seifriz experiment, protoplasm is the test object for the dynamic etheric double, or psychodynamic field. Otherwise, the protoplasm of the slime mold would have picked up its movement where it had left off. Instead, it responded to the dynamic field that was moving in the opposite direction when the anesthesia wore off.

Were it not for anesthesia, we would experience terrible pain during surgery. No doubt everything that our doctors tell us about the way anesthesia works is true. At the same time, it is possible that the unseen etheric double is a link between the physical body and consciousness. Some clairvoyants tell us that when we are anesthetized, they can see that the etheric double is forced a short distance outside of the physical body. That is analogous to the iron filings being moved away from the magnetic field in the bar magnet experiment just described. When the effects of the anesthesia wear off, the "double" returns to place, and once again we can feel pain.

Should we be so unfortunate as to require amputation of a leg, the etheric double of the leg is said to disintegrate after surgery. Yet after amputation, some people experience what has been called a phantom limb. They claim to feel the presence of a leg that is not there. What they may be feeling is the etheric double that has not yet disintegrated. Some doctors note that patients who accept their fate and try to get on with life do not experience much, if any, of the phantom limb syndrome. However, patients who long to have their arm or leg back do "feel" the missing limb. Dora Kunz, the gifted clairvoyant and founder of the healing modality known as Therapeutic Touch, believed that constant thinking about a lost limb actually energizes the etheric double, preventing it from disintegrating rapidly.

According to Dora, the etheric double is a duplicate of the physical body. That duplicate is a kind of force field associated with energy-substance that is invisible to the physical eye. By clairvoyantly observing the etheric double,

Dora could often "see" the source of health problems. She would then advise the patient to seek medical attention if needed. In addition to helping hundreds of patients, Dora also participated in some impressive medical research. For a time she worked with Dr. Shafika Karagulla, a highly qualified neuropsychiatrist. The doctor contributed her medical knowledge to the research, and Dora contributed her clairvoyant ability. Dora's part in the research was to observe the etheric double and report what she saw. Some very dramatic results were produced.

In one experiment at Sloan-Kettering Cancer Center in New York, patients were brought out and placed in the center of the room with their backs to Dora. On one occasion, she observed a highly unusual phenomenon in the etheric double of a patient's brain. She reported that there was a spot in the etheric double of the brain that had no energy whatsoever. It appeared to be a vacuum. Dr. Karagulla asked Dora to point to the spot on the patient's head. Dora did so, and when the medical records were checked, they revealed that a portion of the brain had been excised in that very spot.

The energy that flows through the etheric double and the physical body has been called prana. That vital energy is said to be universal, just as buddhi is universal. The energy itself flows through us, but it is not our body; nor is it the etheric double. It is that which energizes both. Some people are born with an amazingly vital energy flow, while others seem to be born tired. Unlike the physical body, which remains relatively constant, the flow of prana can change rapidly. Most of us have days when we feel full of energy and other days when it is an effort just to make breakfast. The amount of prana that flows through us may be determined by a number of factors. If we are emotionally upset, we may find that our energy is drained. If we are physically ill, our energy level will be affected. Diet, environment, and heredity may all contribute to the amount of energy we have at our disposal.

You can detect the presence of the etheric double and prana by doing a simple experiment. Hold your hands out about a foot in front of your body, elbows at your side, palm facing palm. Now gradually bring your palms together. As you do so, note any subtle changes in feeling in your hands. You may well sense a difference as the palms are brought closer together. Some will feel an opposing force as though they were collapsing a bellows filled with air. Others may have different sensations. You may try the experiment several times, moving your palms together at slightly different speeds each time. If you do detect a sensation of some kind in your palms as you do the experiment, you are probably feeling the prana that is being projected through your etheric double.

The people who detect such a sensation almost as soon as they begin to bring their palms together are often people who have done Therapeutic Touch or some other healing modality. Painters, sculptors, and others who work regularly with their hands also tend to detect a different sensation almost immediately. Most likely that is because they are used to sending energy through their hands, whether or not they have consciously done so.

The etheric double, prana, and kama-manas, all taken together, constitute the human aura that some clairvoyants claim to see. The aura is not something that we have. It is something that we are. What clairvoyants are seeing is the energy-substance that *is* our mental and emotional nature.

It is the constant stream of thought, emotion, and energy swirling through us that is perceived as an aura. According to Dora Kunz, the etheric double extends only a few inches from the physical body. The mental and emotional aura extends out much further. While habitual thoughts and feelings may reveal an identifiable pattern in the aura, these thoughts, feelings, and even our energy are constantly changing. Therefore, like everything else in our universe, the aura is changing every second.

We come now to the final principle, the one with which we are all so familiar: the physical body. Every principle from atma to prana is expressed through the body. We can focus our consciousness, atma, at any point in our body. When we get an insight from buddhi, that insight is flashed on or through our brain. Thinking and understanding through manas involves our brain. Emotions, kama, are expressed through the body. Every principle is revealed through the physical body.

The Buddha taught that enlightenment could only occur during incarnation in the body; Blavatsky and the Hindu sage Shankaracharya have said the same. Perhaps that is because enlightenment is the great flash of insight that reveals how the system works as one whole. That insight flashes through every principle from the source of all to the physical brain. It is only while living in this physical world that such a unifying insight is possible because only while incarnate are all seven principles active in us. As St. Paul wrote, the body is "the temple of the living God" (2 Cor. 6:16).

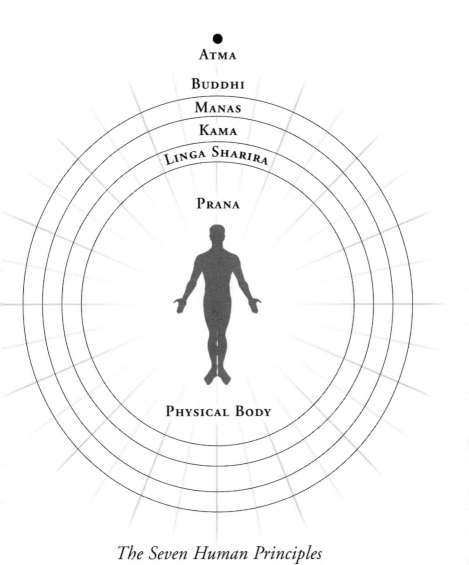

ATMA

BUDDHI

MANAS

KAMA

LINGA SHARIRA

PRANA

PHYSICAL BODY

The Seven Human Principles

Chapter Six

WHAT SURVIVES
DEATH?

I f the body is the temple of the living god, what happens to the living god when the body dies?

Attitudes toward death vary widely from culture to culture and from person to person. Some are convinced that they are nothing more than their body, and therefore when it dies, they die. Those people charge that the idea of life beyond death is nothing more than wishful thinking brought on by a fear of extinction. Other people from every culture believe that somehow we survive physical death. Some of them believe that our soul (whatever that may be) goes to heaven or to hell.

The theories about heaven and hell vary widely. Heaven might be a place quite like earth, except that there are golden streets, no pain, and great joy. Or heaven might be a state of consciousness, a state of bliss. Hell, of course, is a place of punishment and suffering. It, too, can be a nearly physical place with real flames, or it can be a state of consciousness devoid of love and joy.

Perhaps we can never know what death brings until we die ourselves. However, there is some evidence that we can be conscious *outside* of our physical bodies. If that is true, it follows that we might be conscious outside of the body after the body dies. Research on near-death experiences has amassed an impressive body of statistical evidence that points toward such a possibility.

In a near-death experience, all vital signs have ceased. There is no detectable heartbeat or breathing. The body appears to be dead. In some cases it is now possible to resuscitate a person from this near-death condition. Dr. Kenneth Ring of the University of Connecticut is one of the leading researchers on near-death experiences. He has interviewed thousands of people who were brought back from near-death. Some of these people say they remember nothing. However, a great many of them report strikingly similar experiences that occurred while they were clinically dead.

Perhaps the most common of all those experiences is a flashback of the life just lived. Those who have this experience say their entire life flashed before them in a split second. They find it hard to explain. Many feel that this life review gives them some sense of purpose in that life. Long before research into near-death experiences, Theosophical philosophy taught that at death each of us gets a life review—a debriefing, if you will.

For many, next comes an intense light that seems filled with love and peace. Some say this love is more intense than any love they had ever known in life. Images may appear in the light, but these images are almost certainly the product of our conditioning. If we are devout Christians, we may see Jesus. He may even take us up in his arms. If we are devout Jews, however, it would be more likely that we would see an angel, or simply feel God's presence in the light. A Hindu might see Sri Krishna, and so on. The experience of love and peace will be the same for each, but the way the mind pictures it will depend on the cultural and individual point of view.

Often relatives and friends who have died appear to a dying person. Sometimes they beckon the individual to come with them. On other occasions, they say it is not yet time. Whether these images of the dead are real or fancied, we cannot say. What we *can* say is that most of those who are resuscitated report that they had a strong sense of duty to return to physical life. Often they say they would much rather have remained in that peaceful, loving place, but an overwhelming sense of responsibility to a child or some important work drove them to return.

Many near-death experiences might be explained in purely physical terms by the effect of drugs, a brain being deprived of blood and oxygen, falling blood pressure, etc. There is, however, one experience that defies physical explanation. It is the report of conscious experience outside of the body. Compilers of data on near-death experiences tell us that some individuals accurately describe situations that took place at some distance from their comatose bodies. Occasionally, the description is of something that took place in another room, even on another floor of the hospital. If consciousness is merely a by-product of the brain, how could the brain become aware of something that took place outside the reach of the five physical senses? A more likely explanation is that the clinically dead person actually did leave the body and "see" the distant event that they describe.

Near-death experiences are the most convincing evidence we have for the possibility that consciousness may survive physical death. Beyond that, most of us have only theory.

The Theosophical theory of life beyond physical death tells us what happens to our compound nature at death and after. It deals with the gradual disintegration of four of the seven principles. At the moment of death, prana is withdrawn from the body, perhaps at the last breath. Immediately, all agree, the body begins to disintegrate. From the Theosophical point of view, this is because the etheric double has also withdrawn. It is, you will remember, the etheric double that holds the body together from its formation to its death. Eventually the atoms of the body return to the common pool to be recycled and to become part of other bodies, plants, or animals. The consciousness that is the self, however, is said to remain intact. The etheric double disintegrates along with the body, at once if cremated, gradually if buried.

From a Theosophical perspective, those who experience the near-death state have exited the physical body. Their consciousness is then centered in kama-manas. Those who experience intense love and peace are most likely centered in the higher realms of kama-manas. Some people report that they sense that if they were asked any question, the answer would come to them instantly. In those cases it may be that the individual has touched the state we call buddhi-manas.

Just as the physical body disintegrates after death, kama-manas also disintegrates, but much more slowly. The "atoms" of kama-manas also return to the common pool. While the true self cannot reincarnate as an animal, there is a grain of truth in the concept of transmigration. If an individual has lived a life characterized by lust, cravings of every sort, and frequent outbursts of anger, then the emotional "atoms" of kama-manas will gravitate toward the animal kingdom. The true self does not become an animal, but the emotional "remains" may become part of an animal's emotional nature.

Once the body dies, how is it possible that the "me" survives? If we think of our inner principles as nonmaterial fields, we can see that the field may survive the destruction of the matter that reveals its presence. A simple analogy may suffice to illustrate the point. We all know that television waves are present in the same space that we occupy right now. Yet we do not see or sense them. We need a television set to receive those waves and convert them to audible sound and visual images. The fact that we cannot detect the waves is no proof that they are not there. We know that they are there.

The inner self, the mind, and the emotions are actually nonmaterial fields. Our thoughts and feelings are producing waves in those fields. Our brains respond to each and every vibration in the field, just as the TV responds to signals sent from the transmitter. When the television set is destroyed, the field with its waves is not destroyed. Just so, when the body is destroyed, the field remains. The "me" is still there in the very same place at the very same time.

Up to this point, we have some evidence that suggests survival of bodily death. We also have a reasonable field theory that might explain how consciousness may exist without a physical brain to transmit it. From here on, we can only state what Theosophical philosophy teaches about further stages of life after death.

While in essence the Theosophical theory of life after death is uniform, there are some differences among various authors. The writings of H. P. Blavatsky, along with the letters from her teachers that were published as *The Mahatma Letters to A. P. Sinnett*, suggest that there is normally no *direct* contact between the living and the dead. We must remember that at the time the Theosophical Society was formed, spiritualism was extremely popular in the United States and Europe. Mediums were daily trying to make "direct" contact with the dead by bringing visible "spirits" into séance rooms. As one might expect, many of the mediums were con artists or fakes. Others were merely deluded. It is likely, however, that some were genuine. Blavatsky insisted that when the experiences were genuine, what was produced was nothing more than a dead shell of the true person.

Writing at a time of rampant spiritualism, the early Theosophical writers strongly emphasized that there could be no contact between the living and the dead in séances. Yet there is a statement in *The Mahatma Letters* that suggests that while mediums were not contacting the dead, there could still be some kind of nonphysical contact with them. In Letter 18 of *The Mahatma Letters,* the Master Koot Hoomi tells Sinnett that he is mistaken in his belief about communication with the dead. Speaking of the departed, Koot Hoomi writes, "*They can be visited in Spirit,* their Spirit cannot descend and reach us. They attract, they cannot be attracted" (*The Mahatma Letters* 63).

Extraordinary incidents of indirect contact with the departed have been reported worldwide, and while many claims are suspect, many others appear to be valid. One type of indirect contact is often reported in dreams. Not long after the death of a relative or friend, a person may dream of the dead individual. The last physical image we have had of the person will likely have been of an old and frail person. Yet in the dream they are alive, happy, and looking younger. Sometimes we hear them say, "Don't worry. I'm all right." According to some Theosophical writers, the way we appear after death depends largely on the way we "see" ourselves. Usually our self-image is much better than our physical appearance at the time of death. Hence we appear to friends and relatives with the image we have of ourselves. Free from pain and suffering, we are likely to be quite happy.

While we may be free of pain and suffering immediately after death, we may at first be confused, even fearful. Perhaps we are afraid of judgment. Perhaps we feel that we left a mess that our family will have to sort out. Even if we have no fears or major concerns, now that we are free of the body, we must learn to adjust to our new situation. While alive, we spent a great deal of time on purely physical matters. Every morning after getting out of bed, we usually spend a minimum of an hour getting a shower, dressing, and making and eating breakfast. If we are employed, we are likely to spend another half an hour or more getting to work. Even if we work at a computer, we must physically enter data or code. Lunch and dinner will probably take several more hours. Now imagine your life without *any* physical activity whatsoever. Your daily routine has been radically and suddenly changed. The total absence of physical experience alone would require a period of adjustment. Perhaps that is why so many cultures offer prayers for the dead, especially during the period immediately following death.

People die, of course, in all sorts of circumstances and in all sorts of psychological states. For this reason alone, it would be foolish to suppose that everyone would find themselves in the same state after death. Apart from the absence of physical pain, the after-death state is likely to depend a great deal on the subjective state before death. There is no reason to suppose that the simple act of dying will in and of itself grant us eternal joy or sorrow. Neither is it reasonable to suppose that we will suddenly become omniscient. We are still the same old self. We are still "me."

In the period immediately following death, we have not left the earth at all. We are still right here, but now we are within the superphysical states of our own earth. Soon we adjust to and become comfortable with our new environment, but being in a nonphysical state, neither we nor the new environment are visible to physical eyes. What we do there is a subject of debate. Most likely there are a number of possibilities. Whatever may engage us, we gradually shift the focus of our attention from the cares of the past life to the ideals of the past life.

There comes a point when, according to Blavatsky, even the memory of pain is gone. We find ourselves in what might be called a heaven state. But that heaven is not a place. It is a state of mind. The Theosophical term for that heaven state is *devachan*, the "shining place." There are two stages of devachan. The first stage is called the *rupa* (form) stage. The second is the *arupa* (formless) stage. In the first stage, we live out whatever high ideals we may have had during life. It is an intense dream state. Everything seems completely real to us. We see our friends and family, but although we do not realize it, what we see is our image of them.

If during life we had aspired to be an artist or a musician, we can now live out that ideal. We can paint award-winning art, sing on the stage of the Metropolitan Opera, or play a piano on the stage of Carnegie Hall. It would only be in our mind, of course, but we would not know that. The whole experience would be one of happiness and fulfillment. You might say, "Well, if it is imaginary, what is the use of it?" Imaginary it might be, but is it not true that while dreaming, the dream is real and the physical world is not? Only upon awakening do we say, "It was just a dream."

It would appear that if there is any purpose to devachan, it is that by passing through that state we experience a wonderful, delightful rest from the challenges of physical life. It is but another example of the principle of cyclicity. Periods of activity are always followed by periods of rest. That principle runs through the whole of nature, including all the subjective, superphysical states.

We have considered the immediate experiences at death and the first stage of devachan. Before entering the arupa (formless) stage of devachan, all that can be learned from our experiences in life has been absorbed into the inner self, the reincarnating self (buddhi-manas). The old personality with all its faults and habits has gradually disintegrated, leaving only the understanding that has resulted from those experiences. Whatever we have truly learned is not lost. If we have developed musical talent, or if we have developed an ability to understand and work with all sorts of people, that ability becomes part of our character. It comes out as potential in our next life. Some children exhibit great artistic talent. Others can't make a stick figure look good. In the first case, it is likely that the talent was developed in a previous life and reappears as potential in the next. In the other case, most likely there had been little previous interest in the arts.

During the arupa stage of devachan, we no longer identify with Mary, Jack, Susan, or whoever we were in the previous life. At this stage we identify with the inner self that endures through all of its incarnations. Blavatsky says that we then experience intense spiritual bliss that may last from a few years to a few thousand years. This is not a reward for good works, or grace from an exterior God. Rather, it is the result of what we have thought, felt, and done in the past life. If we have aspired to the good, the true, and the beautiful, the energy we put into that will be reaped in devachan as spiritual bliss. If we did not have such aspirations during life, there will be nothing to reap, and we'll simply sleep for an indefinite time before reincarnation occurs.

If the law of cyclicity is universal, then reincarnation in some form seems to be inevitable. The question is, who or what reincarnates? Do Mary, Jack, or Susan reincarnate? They do and they don't. Clearly the body does not reincarnate. Our psychological state changes from childhood to old age. In fact, we are continuously in a state of movement and change, both inwardly and outwardly. The "me" is a process rather than a static state. A process cannot reincarnate. Reincarnation is the effect of causes set into motion in the past.

Most of us can remember when we were five years old. In almost every sense, that five-year-old is now "dead." That child will never reincarnate. Yet all the experience of the child has been absorbed by the inner self. Every action produces an effect, and every effect becomes a new cause. We are creating our next incarnation at this very moment. All the thoughts, feelings, and actions of the current "me" are creating the future one. The new "me" will not be a new self. It will be the result of actions produced by the old self.

If reincarnation is a fact, then why do we not remember past lives? If the Theosophical theory about life after death is correct, then it would be highly unlikely that we would have specific memories. That psyche and that brain did not live before. They could not remember what they never experienced. At the same time, there is a kind of memory retained by the inner self. As mentioned before, lessons learned become part of our character.

While specific and verifiable memories of past lives are rare, there is a kind of unverifiable memory that many of us do experience. It is an affinity for a particular culture.

A woman who now lives in New York was born into an Irish-American, Roman Catholic family. Without any Asian influence in her life, she felt drawn to Buddhism and Taoism as soon as she learned about those traditions. Although her parents took her to church regularly, Christianity never interested her. In addition, from childhood she has had a passionate interest in Chinese art. Her parents could never understand it. When she brought Chinese art home, her parents considered it junk. One possible explanation for the woman's strong feelings is that she had been deeply influenced by Chinese culture in a previous incarnation.

In another case, a man was born into a family with very little education and no interest in culture of any kind. He attended a Protestant church with his grandmother, and when he was old enough he went to every service on his own. His father was an atheist, his mother not in the least religious. The first time the boy saw Catholic ritual he felt completely at home. The lad always had a strong affinity with the Roman Empire and also with medieval Europe, especially England and France. He now lives in the United States. He can discover nothing in his present life that might have produced such strong affinities. He joined the Theosophical Society as a young man—and discovered that a rough estimate of the average time between births is eight hundred years. If he did live in the Roman Empire, medieval Europe, and now the United States, it would be about eight hundred years between each incarnation. This is not proof of reincarnation, but it is powerfully supportive evidence—especially to the man who has had that experience.

In certain cases, the process between incarnations is cut radically short. This is often true when a child dies, or when a young adult is killed. Rather than the usual disintegration of the psyche, that individual may reincarnate with the very same psyche. Therefore, memory of the previous life may be impressed on the new brain. There are many cases on record of individuals who claim they have memories of past lives. Most of them cannot be proven one way or the other. One possible explanation for valid memories of former lives may be cases in which the individual has reincarnated with the same psyche.

In one case a transsexual was asked when she first thought of herself as a woman. She said that it was in a gym class when she was a boy in the first grade. The boys were required to change into shorts for the class, and when she got to the locker room she said to herself, "I can't go in there. I am a woman." Unfortunately, through some anomaly of nature her psyche may have reincarnated in a male body.

Theoretically, we have all amassed a great deal of karmic energy from actions in the past. In our earlier incarnations, we acted out of ignorance, eventually got the reactions, and learned from the experience. We can even see this process in animals. Acting out of ignorance, a cat may put its face too close to a fire and singe its whiskers. That is a learning experience. The cat will not go near that fire again.

The third objective of the Theosophical Society suggests that we investigate the powers latent in humanity. Talents of every kind, clairvoyance, intuition, and most of all the ability to transform ourselves are all latent powers. If we develop a talent in one life, we do not lose the ability at death. In a new incarnation, that ability will reappear as inclination or potential. If we spent long years developing musical talent, we will find ourselves drawn to music in a later life. We will be born with musical talent. Those who have never been involved with music may find musical concepts difficult to understand.

Over many lives, we have learned a great deal, not only from what we have studied, but from the way we have lived. We can choose to live a good life or one of debauchery. We can harbor hatred and suspicion, we can plot against our neighbor, or we can choose to live ethically and in harmony with our neighbors. The actions based on our choices do not necessarily result in immediate reactions. Over many lives the forces set into motion by our intentionality build up what we might call a strong karmic charge that must eventually be neutralized. Many people seem to have an unconscious awareness of this fact. As they approach death, they often try to resolve damaged relationships. Because of deep resentment, a woman may not have spoken to a brother for years. A man may have disowned his mother out of hatred. In each case, the individual may realize that it is important to neutralize the resentment or hatred before they die. Frequently, the moribund person contacts the estranged relative, and healing takes place. Insofar as they have been successful, they have neutralized that bit of their karma so that they will not have to carry it over to a future life.

It is said that, just before we reincarnate, the inner self chooses to work out a portion of that karmic charge in the new incarnation. This gives our new life a profound purpose. Even though our conscious mind may be unaware of it, we are pressured from within ourselves to fulfill that purpose.

Many people don't think about, or even care about, any purpose in life. It is enough to enjoy themselves and to find a good job, a loving mate, and a happy family. "Eat, drink, and be merry" is sufficient for a large number of people. However, at times of crisis, even the most convinced materialist or hedonist often wonders, "Why?" Not knowing where to search for the answer to that most fundamental of all questions, and perhaps believing that it is unanswerable, most return to the customary search for happiness. Only a few begin to search for meaning and purpose.

A Sanskrit name for the inner purpose of life is *dharma*. The word has no adequate English translation, but it has been described in a number of ways. Among them are "duty," "law," "righteousness," "religion," and "essential nature." With the exception of "essential nature," all the English terms tend to suggest some outside authority. Dharma has nothing to do with outer authority. It is an inner pressure that moves us in the best direction to confront and neutralize the selected karmic charge from the past. The Theosophical writer Annie Besant defined dharma as "the inner nature at its current stage of evolution, plus the law of growth for the next stage of evolution" (*Dharma* 21).

Older people who reflect back on their lives sometimes have a sense of their dharma, even if they have never heard the word. They may not be able to articulate it, even to themselves, but they do get a sense that their life has had a purpose and an almost inevitable direction from the beginning. As said earlier, those who have had near-death experiences often report they return to their bodies because of a strong feeling that they must care for their children or complete some unfinished work. That may be simply a sense of responsibility. However, there are cases of children who seem to know that their life has a purpose.

One English girl had a near-death experience at age eleven. She was seated in a dentist's chair awaiting dental work. The dentist covered her nose and mouth with a mask and turned on the gas that would produce a general anesthesia. The mask was not working. The child was nearly asphyxiated. Although she was not religious and had no knowledge of near-death experiences, she suddenly found herself outside her body. She reported that there were other people present asking her to come with them. Her answer to them was, "No. I can't come with you. I have things I must do." At eleven years old she knew that her dharma for that life had not yet been completed. Amusingly, she then thought, "How shall I get back into my body? Head first or feet first?" Then she found herself back in the body. Even in her old age, she never forgot the experience.

Some people believe that we choose our parents before we reincarnate. There may be a grain of truth in that, but only a grain. If we choose to work out a particular chunk of karma, then it is likely that we are automatically incarnated through the parents and the location best suited to provide that opportunity. Once we choose our work for a given incarnation, the stage is set for rebirth through the most appropriate parents.

Working out karma is not an act of penance. We are not punished or rewarded by karma. We are simply experiencing the results of our own past actions and past inaction and learning from the experience. The good or the ill that we have done may place us in a particular family, with people to whom we may be bound by karma. We may come into this life with an inborn talent for music or for mathematics. We may be born with a turbulent or calm emotional nature, or a bright or dull mind. Given our circumstances, we might wonder, what is my dharma in this life?

Annie Besant wrote, "We should be able to discriminate our own dharma by the characteristics which we find in our nature" (*Dharma* 45). Both our talent and our lack of talent determine to some extent where we "belong" in life. It may not be that we are destined to become a professional musician or, for that matter, a plumber. At the same time, if we have those talents, we are likely to use them in some productive way.

We may also discover that circumstances force us to develop strengths that we had not developed in the past. The inner self pushes us to develop in all directions. We tend to develop lopsidedly. We may have great talent in one area and nearly none in another. Some children show great talent for art while others do not. If we can get some sense of our dharma, of what is right for us, obviously we might consciously try to fulfill that dharma. If we do that, we will be working with nature and not against her. We will be making our life more productive and joyful by going with the stream rather than trying to go against it. Sometimes people ask, "Why me?" or, "What am I supposed to learn from this experience?" Such questions are a waste of time. We would do better to pull all our resources together to solve the challenge before us. Only when we have gained new strength and insight are we likely to discover what it was that we had to learn. As the nineteenth-century theologian Søren Kierkegaard once said, "Life is lived forward. It is understood backwards."

By looking backwards, it is possible to get some sense of your dharma by meditating on a few questions.

- Do I feel that what I am doing in life is right?
- Can I see that by being in a particular job or in a particular relationship, I have developed some strength of character that would not have been developed without that job or relationship?
- Can I see how challenges and difficulties have forced me to alter direction and learn from the experience?
- What is it in me that frequently gets me into trouble? Perhaps I am too outspoken, given to angry reactions, or too sentimental. Perhaps I don't know how to say "no" when I should, or I say "no" when I shouldn't.
- What undeveloped talent in me frequently gets me into trouble? Perhaps I find it difficult to organize my thoughts, or I don't know how to form a meaningful relationship.

Our karma has placed us in such situations. It may be our dharma to develop qualities that we have ignored in the past. An old Chinese proverb says, "Pain makes man think. Thinking makes man wise. And wisdom makes life endurable." Replacing the word *pain* with the word *challenge* may be a sensible way to look at our karma and our dharma.

When we fulfill our dharma, or at least as much of it as we can, it is likely that we die. Life's purpose ended, we assimilate the lessons learned and begin a new adventure when we are reborn.

The whole process of reincarnation is but one example of the law of periodicity as expressed in the second fundamental proposition of *The Secret Doctrine*. Everything from microscopic particles to galaxies goes through cycles that reveal an ordered universe.

The books that have been written on reincarnation range from the absurd to the astute. One of the most convincing books on the subject is *European Cases of the Reincarnation Type* by Dr. Ian Stevenson. Dr. Stevenson is intellectually honest. He does not claim proof of reincarnation. Rather, he lists some extraordinary cases of remembered past lives that seem to defy any other explanation. Anyone interested in exploring the possibility of reincarnation will find his work thought provoking.

Chapter Seven

CONSCIOUS EVOLUTION

W e now come to the third fundamental proposition in Blavatsky's *The Secret Doctrine*. That proposition speaks of

> the fundamental identity of all Souls with the Universal Over-Soul [*atma-buddhi*], the latter being itself an aspect of the Unknown Root; and the obligatory pilgrimage for every Soul—a spark of the former—through the Cycle of Incarnation (or "Necessity") in accordance with Cyclic and Karmic law. (*The Secret Doctrine* 1:17)

In this proposition, Blavatsky asserts that we are one with the Oversoul, or atma-buddhi. She then says that as sparks of the Oversoul, all of us pass through an evolutionary process, or pilgrimage, "first by natural impulse, and then by self-induced and self-devised efforts," as Blavatsky goes on to say in this same passage.

Mark Twain once said that every German sentence has all the parts of speech in it, but not in the usual order. He might just as well have been speaking of the matter that became our solar system after the Big Bang. While it is theorized that all the matter here now was there at the Big Bang, it was not ordered as it is now. Our universe does not spring into existence fully formed. Only gradually is the order impressed on matter. The process begins as homogeneous subatomic particles become atoms, molecules, galaxies, and solar systems. Evolution, or progressive development, can be observed in every kingdom of our world. Geological ages preceded the appearance of plants. The animal kingdom developed over many ages, eventually producing mammals. At almost the last minute in geological time, human beings appeared on the scene.

The whole evolutionary process proceeds in an orderly way, in stages and over long epochs. Each stage has identifiable features and characteristics. Each develops what we might call new abilities. For example, plants can do more than rocks in the sense that they have at least some capacity to move. Animals are free to move from place to place, some slowly, others with amazing speed. Unlike rocks and plants, animals have an emotional nature and, to some extent, mental ability. As we move up the evolutionary scale, each kingdom exhibits greater potential, more freedom of action. It is almost as though a new dimension is added to each progressive state without losing what has been gained in the previous kingdom. When we come to human beings, the potential is enormously greater than that of any other kingdom of nature.

All evolutionary theorists agree that the process passes through various identifiable stages. The unanswered question is, "What causes it?" The Theosophical view is that since consciousness and matter are inseparable, they evolve together. Learning takes place through repeated experience in matter of all types. This may not be evident in the mineral kingdom, but it certainly is in the human kingdom. We self-conscious humans act in and through the material world. Our actions at every level produce results, and from the consequences of our actions we eventually learn which actions bring pain and which bring joy.

Furthermore, evolution proceeds from what is inside to what is outside. That is, an inner potential or field impresses its order on substance in the same way that a magnetic field forces iron filings to conform to the pattern of its invisible force. Einstein searched for a unified field theory. While he never found it, it is possible that there is such an all-encompassing field. If so, we might say that the "unified field" is a universal, dynamic field that gradually imposes its order on matter. This is only a hunch to most of us, but it might well be a fact. If so, it would answer many questions related to the evolutionary process.

For example, why does an acorn turn into a giant oak tree? Why does a butterfly emerge from a chrysalis that was once a caterpillar? Or for that matter, why does our earth produce plants, animals, and humans out of the homogeneous substance present at the Big Bang?

The great Belgian philosopher and paleontologist Pierre Teilhard de Chardin seems to have accepted the Theosophical premise that evolution proceeds from inside to outside. He claimed that the saber-toothed tiger had the tooth of a saber-toothed tiger because it had the *soul* of a saber-toothed tiger. In other words, the inner state produced the outer form.

We can see reflections of this theory in ourselves. Our state of mind is often revealed on our face. Perhaps we have arranged to meet a good friend for lunch at a favorite restaurant. As soon as our friend arrives, we take one look at his or her face and we say, "What's wrong?" Without any verbal communication, we know that all is not well simply by the facial expression. When as adults we *habitually* feel joyful, or hostile, the facial muscles will tend to reflect these emotions almost permanently. Of course, we can learn how to mask our feelings by forcing ourselves to look happy when we are not. It does, however, take effort, and even that effort begins with an inner intention.

Since human beings are part of nature, it would follow that we also evolve. It would appear that the physical human form has more or less completed its evolutionary journey. That is, there is no evidence that we may be developing more eyes, ears, or any internal organs. Minor variations may certainly occur, but physically we are not likely to change much in any noticeable way in the future. Although minor variations may occur in the human form, our physical form will probably remain relatively constant. With some exceptions, we all have two eyes and two ears. There is no evidence that evolution will eventually produce humans with four eyes or three ears. Also, it appears likely that there will be no more clever, gifted, talented creatures to appear beyond the human one.

We may have arrived physically, but most assuredly we have not yet fulfilled our psychological and spiritual potential. Some theorists claim that humanity is now evolving psychologically and culturally. This resembles the Theosophical view, which holds that humanity passes through long stages of development.

The early Theosophical writer A. P. Sinnett was taught this theory by one of Blavatsky's teachers, and he was asked to come up with an English term for it. He called each stage a "Root Race." The term can be misleading because when most people hear the word "race," they think of ethnicity. Here the term does not refer to ethnicity but rather to a stage of development.

It is said that there are seven major Root Races, or stages of human development. The first two-and-a-half of these are not physical. Following the concept that evolution proceeds from what is inside to what is outside, the human race does the same. It begins at the most ethereal levels and finally becomes physically incarnate. Each Root Race develops one sense. We have five physical senses, so we are in the fifth Root Race. Along with the physical senses, we develop subjectively. In the fourth Root Race, sometimes called the Atlantean, we developed the emotional nature. The personal ego was formed, giving us a strong sense of "me." We are now developing our mental potential and will probably continue to do so for thousands of years to come.

The next sense to be developed is intuition. The term *intuition* is used to mean insight rather than psychic hunches. From time to time everyone gets a flash of understanding. These flashes of insight seem to come out of nowhere. We don't know how or why we suddenly understand something. Theoretically, over millennia, the human race will develop the ability to have such insights at will. We may learn how to focus our mind on any subject of inquiry so that we instantly understand it. That is nearly impossible for most of us at our current stage of development. But the fact that we all occasionally get such insights is evidence that we have that ability. Mastering it is quite another issue. If and when we do, we will be in the sixth Root Race stage of human development. The seventh stage is so far beyond us that we can only guess what it might be. Suffice it to say that it may have something to do with spiritual will.

Each one of these stages of human development takes many thousands of years. No stage ends abruptly, any more than a child abruptly becomes an adult. When the new developmental stage first appears, the "newcomers" are in a small minority. Gradually they become the norm, and the "old timers" who have not yet begun to develop the new ability, or sense, are in the minority.

Theoretically, all human beings alive today have passed through every major stage of development from what we call the first Root Race to the current fifth Root Race. The first four stages, or races, are not only sequentially developed, they are simultaneously present now. We *are* the first through to the fifth Root Races because we lived through those stages of development, and the abilities perfected in earlier stages are still present with us today. Similarly, the sixth and seventh Root Races are said to be present today. In almost all of us, those Root Races are mere potential. In a few rare individuals, known as adepts, that potential has been fully realized. Therefore, because the Root Races are really stages of development, all seven are present today. Five of them are fully developed in all of us, while the last two have been developed only in a very small minority.

The third fundamental proposition of *The Secret Doctrine* further states that the evolutionary process proceeds "first by natural impulse, and then by self-induced and self-devised efforts." It is at the human stage that "self-induced and self-devised efforts" begin. Up to the human being, evolution goes on without individual self-conscious effort. Theosophically speaking, we can say that fish did not one day make a conscious decision to crawl up onto the land, grow legs, and breathe air. Somehow land animals appeared. As previously stated, we humans have almost certainly reached the end of physical evolution. It is what makes us human that may be evolving by self-induced effort.

Modern psychology assures us that we can solve many of our psychological problems if we make the effort to do so. Despite the widespread use of antidepressants, psychiatrists still cannot prescribe a pill that will solve all of our problems. We must see what it is that we are doing that makes us unhappy. Then we must positively change our thought patterns and behavior. We can only "cure" ourselves. No one can do it for us. If we do not want to change, we will not change. Human evolution will remain nearly stagnant unless we decide to change, to develop, to seek our innermost nature and to direct our life from that center.

Often the desire, or indeed the necessity, for change comes from conflict. As a prominent Theosophist once said, "Comfort does not beget change." When we are content, we are not inspired to change. On the other hand, when we face difficult circumstances, we usually do our best to seek a resolution. Some theorists suggest that "conflict resolution" may be what brings about psychological and cultural evolution. This is similar to the Theosophical theory. Two major world tragedies may provide some evidence on its behalf.

After the First World War, many nations looked for resolution. They formed the League of Nations. It was an effort to think and work globally. It was not very effective. The Second World War was soon upon us, and the shock of such a terrible conflict awakened a new and stronger desire to prevent future catastrophes. The United Nations was formed. It has lasted longer than the League of Nations, and even though it is far from perfect, it has been instrumental in resolving some conflicts.

When people who have reached middle age look back on their lives, they can often see that they have learned most from their difficult experiences. Peaceful and happy times are important and necessary, but it appears that real change, real learning, comes out of dealing with the challenges we meet.

Blavatsky and her teachers tell us that in many thousands of years the whole human race will have developed its potential to the fullest. Evolution proceeds slowly. This is true of human evolution as well as the evolution of the planet. We do not change ourselves rapidly. We have to work at it. After beginning to develop our inner potential, we may find that further development can be achieved more rapidly, but it will always require self-induced and self-devised effort. A humorous tale may illustrate the point.

Mrs. Doolittle lived in a flood zone, but her home was on a small hill and had never been severely affected by occasional floods. One year an unusually severe flood was predicted as all but certain. The authorities required everyone in the affected towns to evacuate, and that included Mrs. Doolittle. A policeman asked Mrs. Doolittle to evacuate, but she replied, "God will take care of me," and she stayed put. As the water rose to her porch, authorities in a boat came by and asked Mrs. Doolittle to come aboard to safety. She repeated that God would take care of her. The water rose still higher, and she found herself sitting on the roof. A helicopter came by, lowered a ladder, and asked her to climb to safety. Once again, she said, "God will take care of me." At that, she slipped into the water and drowned. Reaching heaven, she marched up to God and angrily said,

"I had faith that you would take care of me, but you didn't help me at all." God replied, "Mrs. Doolittle, first I sent a policeman; then I sent a boat; then I sent a helicopter."

Others can provide help, but if we refuse to make any effort to "save" ourselves, if we depend on someone else to do it for us, we will surely drown.

Chapter Eight

BEYOND
GOOD AND EVIL

Perhaps the most powerful drive in all living beings is what we call the survival instinct. One need only observe plants and animals to discover ingenious ways in which life strives to complete its natural cycle. We humans are also endowed with a drive to live life to its fullest, but in us it expresses itself not only as physical self-preservation, but also as a search for happiness. And that search for happiness is in reality a longing for self-fulfillment.

Although most of us do find some happiness in life, we soon discover that we can never experience constant happiness. Even relatively contented people experience sorrow in some form, and although we may experience long happy periods in our lives, eventually pleasure gives way to pain, happiness to sorrow. And the reverse is also true.

Both the drive to seek happiness and the impossibility of maintaining it in a constant state are absolutely without exception. They are, from a Theosophical perspective, evidence of two universal principles, unity and polarity.

To get some understanding of these principles, it is helpful once again to consider the beginning—not our own beginning, but the beginning of the universe.

If the universe is to arise out of boundless space, that space must be differentiated. It must "congeal" in places, and when it does, there is contrast between the congealed places and boundless space and between one congealed place and another. Those "congealed" places are matter and hence form. Eternal, undifferentiated space has now become space and substance, nonmaterial and material. There is now contrast. The Eternal has limited itself.

As soon as the universe polarizes, primordial, manifested unity is transformed into plurality. The One becomes the many.

We might ask the ultimate question, "Why does the One polarize and become the manifested universe?" We simply do not know. All we can say is that it appears to be the nature of reality itself.

The breaking asunder of primordial unity has been mythologized in various ways in the great religious traditions. In Christianity, it is "the Lamb, slain from the foundation of the world, dying in very truth that we might live" (*The Liturgy of the Liberal Catholic Church* 215; cf. Rev. 13:8). That "sacrifice" gives us life. Without it, we would be but a potential within the Eternal.

From the very beginning, this primordial sacrifice sets up the principle of polarity. It gives us the polar opposites of space and substance, of inner life and outer form, positive and negative, and of all other polarities that derive from that initial polarization of the One.

Creation myths often begin with homogeneity, frequently symbolized as water. Then the water is somehow divided, giving birth to life and form. The Genesis myth is of that type. An echo of the unity-to-diversity theme also appears in the myth of Adam and Eve. In the Garden of Eden, Adam and Eve are together and all is paradise. Then Eve eats of the Tree of Knowledge, and she suddenly knows good from evil. The One has been rent asunder, giving rise to polar opposites.

What is the connection between eating of the Tree of Knowledge and polarity? Why is Eve the one who first eats of the tree? In the myth, Eve represents matter. Matter is essential to consciousness. If there were no matter, there would be nothing to be conscious *of.* Matter is essential if consciousness is to "know" anything. Matter is "feminine" because it is through matter that consciousness is born. Therefore it is Eve who eats of the Tree of Knowledge, and since it is matter that limits the Eternal, matter has erroneously been associated with evil. It is this sublime truth that has been in past centuries degraded into the absurd idea that women are the cause of evil.

Thus, in order to know, there must be contrast, limitation, polarity. From the polarity of Adam and Eve and all other polarities, we now come to the greatest polarity of all—that of good and evil.

Unlike some religions, Theosophy denies the existence of evil as an independent power, either personified in a devil, or as an aspect of impersonal nature. Koot Hoomi, one of Blavatsky's adept teachers, writes:

> Evil has no existence *per se* and is but the absence of
> good and exists but for him who is made its victim. It

proceeds from two causes, and no more than good is it an independent cause in nature. Nature is destitute of goodness or malice; she follows only immutable laws. (*The Mahatma Letters* 273)

As for what we commonly call evil—that is, human evil—the adept writes:

The real evil proceeds from human intelligence and its origin rests entirely with reasoning man who dissociates himself from Nature. Humanity, then, alone is the true source of evil. Evil is the exaggeration of good, the progeny of human selfishness and greediness. Think profoundly and you will find that . . . the *origin* of every evil whether small or great is in human action. . . . Therefore it is neither nature nor an imaginary Deity that has to be blamed, but human nature made vile by *selfishness*. (*The Mahatma Letters* 273–74)

Koot Hoomi goes on to say that religion is a great cause of human evil, but still the root is selfishness and ignorance masking as religion:

Ignorance created Gods and cunning took advantage of the opportunity. . . . It is religion that makes [a human being] the selfish bigot, the fanatic that hates all mankind out of his own sect without rendering him any better or more moral for it. . . . Is not man ever ready to commit any kind of evil if told that his God or Gods demand the crime . . . ? (*The Mahatma Letters* 274)

To say that religion is a major cause of human evil is not to say that there is no good in religious scriptures, rites, or in the followers of any major faith. On the contrary, Koot Hoomi has quoted from various religious texts to illustrate a point with which he agrees. It is not the truths that are often found in scriptures that are evil; it is the "selfish bigot, the fanatic" who often demands control over the faithful and their money. It is human beings who have, at least in many cases, turned religion into an evil. Moreover, is it not true that the cultures of the world have their origin in one or another religion? And is it not true that many of our wars are the direct result of cultural clashes? Even if we no longer believe in a religion, we live in a culture that is based on a religion. We then identify with that culture, and, to paraphrase Koot Hoomi, we run the risk of hating all mankind out of our own culture without making ourselves any the better for it.

Siddhartha Gautama, the Buddha, taught that all human suffering arises out of ignorance. It should be obvious to most of us that ignorance of certain facts about nature would cause suffering. Before the human race was aware of the existence of bacteria, no connection was seen between unsanitary conditions and disease. Suffering and death often resulted from that ignorance. However, the Buddha had something far more fundamental in mind when he said that suffering arises out of ignorance. It is ignorance of our true nature, ignorance of who and what we really are, ignorance of the ground of our own being.

The fact is that consciousness focused in material form tends to identify itself with that form. When we identify with the physical body, for all practical purposes we *are* the physical body, and we do what it wants. What we call the

drive for self-preservation enters in, and we strive to preserve the self that we believe to be only our body. Selfishness, therefore, is a natural consequence of the principle
of self-preservation and our conviction that the self is the
physical body. From this view, selfishness is inevitable. As
may be seen, it is also an essential ingredient in the evolutionary process, even though that inevitable selfishness
results in what we call evil.

Why, then, does evil exist? While we may not ultimately be able to answer that question, we can see that evil
may play a very definite role in evolutionary development.
On this subject Annie Besant writes:

> For their development it is necessary for positive qual-
> ities to be exercised against opposition. Without oppo-
> sition no development is possible; without opposition
> no growth is possible. All growth and development
> result from the exercise of energy against something
> which opposes. (*The Spiritual Life* 109)

That is obviously true of the physical body. Should we
decide never to use our arms, they would wither away. It is
only by using them against the opposition of some weight
that our muscles develop.

It is also easy to see that mental development occurs by
using the mind. Without challenging questions, the mind
tends to function only in habitual ways. Challenges in life
provide the resistance the mind needs to develop. Great
minds, like great athletes, develop by making an effort to
overcome challenges.

What we are less likely to notice is that emotional
development also occurs by overcoming resistance. In the

Tarot deck, which has long been regarded as an embodiment of esoteric wisdom, the first card is the Fool. One of the most common versions of this deck pictures the Fool as a young man on a journey. He is traveling by foot, and while he travels he is looking up with a happy face. What he does not realize is that he is about to step off a cliff.

Like the Fool on the Tarot card, we all set out to seek happiness. Yet in our ignorance we step off a cliff and suffer pain. For example, through ignorance we fall into all sorts of difficulty with other people. Our family, friends, or employers may act in ways that upset us. Not knowing how best to handle the situation, we often make matters worse. Strangers may annoy us, but we can usually walk away from them. Closer relationships cannot be escaped so simply. We must overcome the challenges we meet at work or at home because often we have no other choice. That very fact forces us to develop qualities that will enable us to deal with the difficulty we face. If we are at work and cannot easily resign, we must learn how to deal with our supervisor and peers. In an effort to end our emotional distress, we may search for inner strength, resulting in more patience, courage, tact, and even compassion. Without any emotional resistance, we have no need to strengthen our inner nature. However much we might like to become strong physically, emotionally, and mentally, we cannot do so without working against something that opposes.

St. Augustine realized that evil had a purpose in human life. He writes:

Do not think that the evil are in the world for no purpose, and that God makes no good use of them. Every wicked person lives either that he may be corrected, or that through him the righteous may be tried and tested. (*Exposition on the Psalms* Ps. 55)

St. Augustine also recognized something of that first and greatest principle in Theosophy: the ultimate unity of the whole. Of human unity he goes on to write:

> Would that those who now test us were converted and tried with us; yet though they continue to try us, let us not hate them, for we do not know whether any of them will persist to the end in their evil ways. And most of the time, when you think you are hating your enemy, you are hating your brother without knowing it. (*Exposition* Ps. 55)

The fall of consciousness into matter results in limitation and form, and identification with the limited form results in selfishness and evil. By providing opposition, evil can be useful in the development of human potential.

In our long evolutionary journey, it is that human potential that is being developed. The driving force of self-preservation and the longing for happiness, the inner urge for self-fulfillment, forces us into action. Identified with form, we act out of ignorance. Our actions bring reactions, frequently producing consequences that we did not anticipate, and we learn bit by bit how things truly are. The veil of ignorance is gradually torn away and we perceive that we are *in* the world of opposites, but not *of* it. We discover that we are "the Other," the inner self, the still point beyond good and evil. Blavatsky refers to that still point when she writes:

To reach the knowledge of that SELF, thou hast to give up *Self* to Non-Self, Being to Non-Being, and then thou canst repose between the wings of the GREAT BIRD. Aye, sweet is rest between the wings of that which is not born, nor dies, but is the AUM throughout eternal ages. (*The Voice of the Silence* 5)

In *Leaves of Grass,* Walt Whitman speaks of the experience beyond opposites:

Trippers and askers surround me,
People I meet . . . the effect upon me of my early
    life . . . of the ward and city I live in . . . of the
    nation,
The latest news . . . discoveries, inventions,
    societies . . . authors old and new,
My dinner, dress, associates, looks, business,
    compliments, dues,
The real or fancied indifference of some man or
    woman I love,
The sickness of one of my folks—or of myself . . . or
    ill-doing . . . or loss or lack of money . . . or
    depressions or exaltations,
They come to me days and nights and go from
    me again,
But they are not the Me myself.

Apart from the pulling and hauling stands what I am,
Stands amused, complacent, compassionating, idle,
    unitary,
Looks down, is erect, bends an arm on an impalpable
    certain rest,
Looks with its sidecurved head curious what will come
    next,

Both in and out of the game, and watching and
    wondering at it

Backward I see in my own days where I sweated
    through fog with linguists and contenders,
I have no mockings or arguments . . . I witness and
    wait.

I believe in you my soul . . . the other I am must not
    abase itself to you,
And you must not be abased to the other.

Then, describing the response that flows from such a realization, he writes:

Swiftly arose and spread around me the peace and joy
    and knowledge that pass all the art and argument
    of the earth;
And I know that the hand of God is the elderhand of
    my own,
And I know that the spirit of God is the eldest brother
    of my own,
And that all the men ever born are also my brothers . . .
    and the women my sisters and lovers,
And that a kelson of the creation is love . . . (*Leaves of
Grass* 28–29)

Polarity is an absolutely universal law. Without it, there
would be no universe. We would not exist. With it, we
struggle. Trapped in the illusions of form produced by
polarity and driven by self-preservation and the pursuit of
happiness, we act out of ignorance and selfishness. Then at
last, by the constant lawful consequences of our actions, we

realize that "our hearts are ever restless till they find their rest in Thee," the Eternal.

Those whose meditation is fired by the inexpressible longing of the inner self for the Infinite will know something of that still point for themselves. They will have had the experience that Whitman describes. Yet the fleeting eternity in meditation is only the beginning, for ultimately it must flood our whole being.

Chapter Nine

BLAVATSKY AND THE
THEOSOPHICAL SOCIETY

Now that we have sketched out some of the basic teachings of Theosophy, it would be helpful to go back and look at the life of H. P. Blavatsky, followed by some brief history of the Theosophical movement as a whole.

Helena Petrovna Blavatsky (1831–1891) was born on August 12, 1831, at Ekaterinoslav, Ukraine, Russia. Her father was Colonel Peter Alexeyevich von Hahn, and her mother was Helena Andreyevna, née de Fadeyev, a renowned novelist. In 1849 Helena Petrovna married a much older man, Nikifor Vassilyevich Blavatsky. Not long after the marriage, she left him and soon began extensive travels to many countries in search of metaphysical lore and ancient wisdom. Her travels included time spent in Turkey, Egypt, France, Greece, Mexico, Syria, Italy, Central and South America, Ceylon (now Sri Lanka), India, Burma, and Tibet. In the nineteenth century, that was an astounding and difficult thing for a woman traveling alone to do.

As a child, Helena exhibited amazing psychic abilities. At first she had little control over her psychic powers, but as a young adult she gained full control over them. Extraordinary eyewitness accounts of her psychic ability are recorded in such books as *The Esoteric World of Madame Blavatsky*, by Daniel Caldwell, and *H.P.B.: The Extraordinary Life and Influence of Helena Blavatsky*, by Sylvia Cranston. But Blavatsky was never interested in psychic powers for their own sake. Rather, she sought to understand the principles and natural laws behind them. One of the reasons for her extensive travels was to discover those laws.

Blavatsky has always been a controversial figure. From childhood on, she was extremely outspoken, a characteristic not admired in children, especially girls. As an adult, she continued to make herself unpopular with some by speaking out against hypocrisy and bigotry, two sins that she could never tolerate.

Numerous articles and books have been written about Madame Blavatsky. As might be expected, some of them are laudatory and some accuse her of being a fraud. While Blavatsky was not without faults, there is no evidence that she was a fraud. Most of the charges against her were based solely on rumor. In *Madame Blavatsky's Baboon*, for example, Peter Washington writes that Blavatsky linked nudism to dietary reform, occult wisdom, and universal brotherhood. Yet nowhere in the writings of Blavatsky is there any mention of nudism. Another common rumor is that Blavatsky had an illegitimate child. However, there are medical records stating that she was incapable of bearing any child.

In 1875 Blavatsky, Colonel Henry Steel Olcott, and others formed the Theosophical Society in New York City. The Society has always been open to anyone in sympathy with its objectives, stated in the introduction of this book. Since Theosophy is not a religion, the Society is composed of members from every religious tradition. The Society does not ask people to give up their religion. Rather, it encourages them to search deeply within their own religion for the ancient wisdom that lies within their scriptures and traditions.

Blavatsky was a prolific writer. Her *Collected Writings* fill fifteen volumes. Major works include *Isis Unveiled, The Secret Doctrine, The Voice of the Silence,* and *The Key to Theosophy.* Directly or indirectly, Blavatsky has attracted the attention of great minds in many fields, including science, art, literature, and education. Many have been impressed enough to join the Theosophical Society. Some prominent individuals in these fields who have done so are L. Frank Baum, author of *The Wizard of Oz;* Sir William Crookes, theoretical physicist and inventor; Thomas Edison, American inventor; the Dutch painter Piet Mondrian; Maria Montessori, educator and founder of the Montessori Method; Jawaharlal Nehru, first prime minister of India; Henry Wallace, United States vice-president under Franklin Roosevelt; and the Irish poet William Butler Yeats.

Blavatsky became an American citizen in 1878. She was the first Russian woman to do so. In 1879 she and Olcott went to India, where they established the international headquarters of the Theosophical Society in Madras, now named Chennai.

Henry Steel Olcott (1832–1907), cofounder of the Theosophical Society, was well known in his own right.

He was an agriculturist, a lawyer, a journalist, and a colonel in the Union Army during the Civil War. He was assigned to investigate fraud in the New York Mustering and Disbursement Office and also in the Navy Yards in Washington, D.C. When Abraham Lincoln was assassinated, Olcott was appointed to a three-man panel to investigate the crime.

While president of the Theosophical Society, Olcott traveled to Sri Lanka, then named Ceylon. There he worked for the oppressed Buddhist population. He even produced a Buddhist catechism, one that all groups of Buddhists could accept. In Sri Lanka, Olcott is a national hero. There are statues of him in prominent places, and there is even a postage stamp in his honor.

Blavatsky and Olcott toured northern India in 1879, where they met and stayed with Mr. and Mrs. A. P. Sinnett in Allahabad. Sinnett was the editor of *The Pioneer*, India's foremost newspaper at the time. He published reports about their mission in India, but soon this became so burdensome that in October of 1879 Blavatsky founded *The Theosophist*. That journal is still being published by the Society at its headquarters in Adyar.

Early in 1885, Blavatsky began to write her major work, *The Secret Doctrine*. Soon, however, she became seriously ill. At the time Olcott was on tour in Burma, but when he learned of her illness he returned to India. Blavatsky's doctor warned her that staying in the hot Indian climate could be disastrous for her. Although she preferred to stay in India, she traveled to Europe and settled at Würzburg, Germany. It was there that she began work on *The Secret Doctrine* in earnest. After Blavatsky left India, Olcott established a library on the Society's estate. That library still functions today as a major center for the study of Asian religions. In 1892 Olcott wrote *Old Diary Leaves*, a history of the Theosophical Society that included many of his experiences with Blavatsky and others during his work for the Society.

From Würzburg Blavatsky moved on to Ostend, Belgium. While working on *The Secret Doctrine* she became seriously ill again. Her doctor was certain that she would die within twenty-four hours after he saw her. Strangely, she awoke the next morning in apparently excellent health. Blavatsky claimed that one of the adepts had come in the night to tell her that she could die and take her reward, or she could be "patched up" for a short time so that she could finish *The Secret Doctrine.* She chose to stay on for a while longer, and the adept used his knowledge and ability to heal her. In May of 1887 she moved to London, where she completed her work and died on May 8, 1891. The Theosophical Society around the world celebrates her death each year on or near May 8 as White Lotus Day.

While Blavatsky gave the world a modern statement of Theosophy, Olcott organized the Theosophical Society. Blavatsky had very little organizing talent. Without her we would not have had modern Theosophy, but without Olcott we would not have had the Theosophical Society to preserve and promulgate Theosophical concepts.

After the death of Olcott in 1907, Annie Besant became president of the Society. In addition to helping to popularize Theosophy, Besant worked tirelessly with Gandhi and others to free India from British rule. This resulted in her becoming the first president of the Congress Party, a home-rule party. She became so well known in India that many Indians think of the Theosophical Society as "Annie

Besant's Society." There is a statue of her in Chennai near the beach, and avenues and shops are named after her. Since Besant's death in 1933, there have been five more presidents elected to office. They, along with many others, have made a contribution to Theosophical thought and literature. The Society's Olcott Library in Wheaton, Illinois, contains many volumes on Theosophy and related subjects. In addition, there are libraries in numerous branches of the Society around the world.

Since the founding of the Theosophical Society in 1875, branches have been established in nearly seventy countries. In addition, several independent groups that broke from the parent organization have established centers for the study of Theosophy.

In the early days of the Theosophical Society, Blavatsky claimed that she was being tutored by two extraordinary Eastern teachers whose names were Morya and Koot Hoomi. At first, she alone claimed to have seen these men. Because of that, many wondered if they were real. Some thought that they were figments of Blavatsky's imagination. Others thought that they must be divine, or at least other than human. In an attempt to separate fiction from fact, the next chapter will present what Blavatsky had to say about them and what they had to say about themselves.

Chapter Ten

THE MAHATMAS AND
THEIR LETTERS

The word *mahatma* means "great soul." The term has been applied to the individuals that Blavatsky calls adepts, but since it is a title rather than a name, it has been applied to others as well. For example, Mohandas Gandhi was often referred to as Mahatma Gandhi. However great Gandhi may have been, neither he nor Blavatsky herself were adepts or mahatmas in the Theosophical sense. Blavatsky defines a mahatma as

> a personage, who, by special training and education, has evolved those higher faculties and has attained that spiritual knowledge which ordinary humanity will acquire after passing through numberless series of reincarnations during the process of cosmic evolution. . . . The real Mahatma is not his physical body but that higher *Manas* which is inseparably linked to the *Atma* and its vehicle [*Buddhi*]. (*Collected Writings* 6:239)

In Theosophical literature the mahatmas have also been called adepts, the brothers, and the masters. Because among Christians the term "master" tends to be associated with Jesus, it is important to note that Blavatsky used "master" in the sense of "schoolmaster"—a teacher, not a god.

Although mahatmas are relatively few in number, Blavatsky claimed that in her day there were one to two thousand living in various parts of the world. She claimed to have personal acquaintance with several of them, Morya and Koot Hoomi in particular. She said that those two lived beyond the Himalayas. Although they rarely made themselves known to individuals, sometimes they did travel beyond the Himalayas. Blavatsky says that Koot Hoomi traveled to Japan and China every two years, and Morya sometimes traveled to India. She claims that Morya once spent a week in Bombay and that he came to visit her and Olcott twice at that time. Olcott verified her account and said that he saw Morya in his physical body on several other occasions.

Blavatsky tells us that Morya was born a Rajput and Koot Hoomi was born a Kashmiri Brahmin. Neither she nor they ever revealed their personal history. From all they say about themselves in their letters, and from all that Blavatsky wrote about them, they seem to prefer to work outside of public view.

Blavatsky's experience with the masters has provoked much controversy over the years. While many people believe what Blavatsky and Olcott said about the masters, others are convinced that either they never existed, or they were based on the life of men who Blavatsky may have known. In his book *The Masters Revealed*, for example, K. Paul Johnson theorizes that Morya and Koot Hoomi

were no more than cover names for two historical characters, Ranbir Singh and Thakar Singh. However, several crit-
ics have pointed out that Johnson seems to rely only on
circumstantial coincidences to support his theory. Johnson
rejects eyewitness accounts as false, but he seems to do so
merely to prove his thesis. Letters were received from Koot
Hoomi after the death of Thakar Singh, and at least one after
the death of Blavatsky. Those facts alone cast serious doubt
on Johnson's theory. In addition, Thakar Singh was an active
revolutionary. Koot Hoomi and Morya claim only to *influence* people, never to use force to obtain their goals.

Blavatsky claims on one occasion to have visited Morya
and Koot Hoomi in Sikkim. Johnson presents no explanation for Blavatsky's claim, nor for a letter from Koot Hoomi
that corroborates the visit. In that letter, Koot Hoomi wrote:

> I do not believe I was ever so profoundly touched by
> anything I witnessed in all my life as I was with
> [Blavatsky's] ecstatic rapture, when meeting us recent-
> ly both in our [physical] bodies. . . . Even our phleg-
> matic M[orya] was thrown off his balance by such an
> exhibition—of which he was chief hero. He had to use
> his *power* and plunge her into a profound sleep, other-
> wise she would have burst some blood vessel . . . in her
> delirious attempts to flatten her nose against his riding
> mantle besmeared with the Sikkim mud! (*The
> Mahatma Letters* 297)

Blavatsky's first encounter with Morya was by psychic
means when she was a child. She claims that she often had
visions of a tall Indian man, but she did not know his name.
She said that for some reason she thought that he was

watching over her. Later she learned that he simply called himself Morya.

Although the account is not verifiable in every detail, Blavatsky said that in 1851 she was in London at the time of the Great Exhibition, a kind of world's fair. During a parade that included delegations from all around the British Empire, she saw Morya in one of the delegations. One can imagine the intense emotion that she must have experienced when she saw the man of her vision physically before her. She rushed into the street, but Morya waved her back.

The next day Blavatsky met Morya in Hyde Park, where he told her that for some time he and a colleague by the name of Koot Hoomi Lal Singh had been searching for someone who might be suited to bring their teachings to the West. Morya explained that although Blavatsky had many faults, they had chosen her as the most likely candidate for such an assignment. He told her that if she accepted the mission, she would gain nothing personally. She would have little money and would not profit one cent from the work offered her. Her health was poor and would not get better. In presenting their ideas to the West, she would be attacked by clergy and scientists. Friends would betray her, and in general life was not going to be easy. The choice, Morya said, was hers. She could help to lift some of the veil of ignorance from humanity if she was willing to accept the sacrifices it would require. She accepted, and it all came true. Her health deteriorated. At her death she did not leave enough to pay for her own funeral. She was attacked and betrayed often. However, her dedication and unselfish nature prevailed.

For over a hundred years, people have wondered whether the adepts were figments of Blavatsky's imagination or living men. If we had no other evidence for the existence of these two extraordinarily wise and knowledgeable men, Blavatsky's writings would be sufficient to convince many reasonable people that they did indeed exist, and that they were her teachers. Her major work, *The Secret Doctrine*, is a remarkable body of thought on science, religion, and philosophy. It is an overwhelming document that leaves most students wondering how she, or anyone else, could have gathered such an impressive body of knowledge.

Blavatsky said that what she taught was a portion of the accumulated wisdom of the ages, preserved and passed on by great adepts from the very dawn of humanity. Although she gathered some of that knowledge herself, she claimed that the bulk of her teachings were given to her by Morya and Koot Hoomi. Blavatsky was convinced that some, if not all, of the most fundamental teachings of the adepts would be validated by science in the twentieth century. Apparently, she was not far from wrong, because some aspects of the three fundamental propositions of *The Secret Doctrine* have now been validated by modern science. One case in point is her teaching about the nature of matter.

In the late 1800s Blavatsky said that the cornerstone of Theosophical philosophy rests upon the illusory nature of matter and the infinite divisibility of the atom. The physicists of her day were convinced that matter consisted of little indivisible billiard-ball atoms, banging into one another all over the universe. Since her time, that "indivisible" atom has been split, and frequently new subatomic particles are discovered. Today physicists openly admit that matter is not what it appears to be. The nature of matter is illusory and the atom can be split.

Blavatsky was a cultivated Russian noblewoman, but she was not a scientist. How could she have known that the atom was divisible when the scientists of her day said that it was not? If she discovered such scientific facts on her own, then she must have been as amazing an individual as the adepts who taught her. The fact that the adepts knew that the atom is divisible suggests that human beings may be able to discover truth by methods other than those employed by contemporary scientists.

Were there no other evidence for the existence of adepts, *The Secret Doctrine* alone would suggest that they did and possibly still do exist. However, we do have other evidence.

A. P. Sinnett evinced strong interest in Blavatsky's teachers. He wanted to know just who they were and what they taught, and he wanted to know it directly from them. So in 1880 he initiated a lengthy correspondence with Morya and Koot Hoomi. Those letters are available in book form, entitled *The Mahatma Letters to A. P. Sinnett.* (Some passages from them have already been quoted.) The original letters are currently in the manuscript division of the British Library in London.

Blavatsky had been falsely accused of forging the letters, and as is usual with rumors, many believed the lie. The Society for Psychical Research launched an investigation that was conducted by Dr. Richard Hodgson. In his report, Hodgson branded Blavatsky as a fraud. The investigation was so biased and so shoddy that nearly one hundred years later the same society revisited the case and declared that Hodgson's conclusions were not supportable. In their revised report the society stated that Blavatsky "could *not* have written the specimens of Mahatma calligraphy submitted for examination." In effect, the society washed its hands of the case (Waterman 47).

In these letters, Morya and Koot Hoomi presented something of their philosophical and scientific ideas. They also explained to Sinnett that while they were indeed human, they had developed the human potential to a far greater degree than had the vast majority of the race. While they may enjoy far better physical health than most of us, they are still human beings. Their occult powers and their knowledge of nutrition may enable them to live for several centuries, but they do not live for thousands of years. Eventually the body wears out, and from what they say, when it does, they consciously discard it. Whether or not Morya and Koot Hoomi have taken a new incarnation or remain in the same physical body today is not known.

The physical body of an adept does not differ greatly from ours. Therefore, in the highly unlikely event that we should meet an adept, we would be unaware of any difference between such an individual and any healthy person that we might meet.

In many ways, all human beings are similar to one another. We do not look very different, and in many ways we do not act differently. Yet inwardly we differ far more than may at first meet the eye. There are vast differences of development in intellect among human beings. There are also great differences in artistic ability. One person can hardly carry a tune, while another can audition for the Metropolitan Opera. The integrity of individuals also varies enormously. There are vast differences in character: some are highly sensitive, some crude and uncultivated. Spiritually, who knows how different we all are?

The adepts say that human potential is enormously greater than most of us have imagined. They claim to have developed that potential to such a high degree that they have access to what Koot Hoomi calls "every first truth." They claim to have discovered the laws that govern our solar system, both objectively and subjectively. Their powers to manipulate matter and energy appear to be miraculous, yet they say that everything they do is governed by natural law. They have learned those laws by centuries of study, experience, and testing.

An adept is the fully developed inner self. As such, an adept is neither male nor female. St. Paul wrote, "There is neither Jew nor Greek, there is neither bond nor free, there is neither male nor female: for ye are all one in Christ Jesus" (Gal. 3:28). Perhaps St. Paul knew that at the level of buddhi we are all one. Surely the phrase "in Christ" does not mean *belief* in Christ. All Christians believe in Christ, yet they have killed one another over theological and other disagreements. Belief does not make us one. If, however, we are centered in buddhi, we are one.

There are reports that adepts have taken both male and female bodies. The teachers of Blavatsky took male bodies, as many have. We can only guess why they seem to have incarnated as men more often than women. One possibility is that they knew that for many centuries people would not accept a female teacher. That may change in the future.

The adepts claim to teach only what they know from personal experience and from centuries of testing and verification by other adepts. They even say that if any adept claims to have discovered a truth, it will not be accepted until it can be corroborated by other adepts. They claim that their personal knowledge extends only to the laws of our solar system. While they cannot verify anything outside of our solar system, they assume that the laws do not break down beyond it.

Moreover, they claim that every human being is potentially capable of doing what they can do, but not without one-pointed purpose, study, and most of all, self-transformation. The process for reaching such a level of development requires, according to them, not weeks or years, but many lifetimes. Yet they encourage all to begin the long process by trying.

Since Blavatsky introduced the adepts to the general public, understandable misconceptions about their nature have arisen. Let's consider what they have to say about themselves.

In an effort to clear up some misconceptions about their nature, Koot Hoomi wrote:

> An adept—the highest as the lowest—is one *only during the exercise of his occult powers*. ... Whenever these powers are needed, the sovereign will unlocks the door to the *inner* man (the adept). (*The Mahatma Letters* 257)

Regarding the exercise of those occult powers, he writes:

> The smallest exercise of occult powers ... requires an effort. We may compare it to the inner muscular effort of an athlete preparing to use his physical strength. As no athlete is likely to be always amusing himself at swelling his veins in anticipation of having to lift a weight, so no adept can be supposed to keep his will in constant tension and the *inner* man in full function,

when there is no immediate necessity for it. When the *inner* man rests the adept becomes an ordinary man, limited to his physical senses and the functions of his physical brain. Habit sharpens the intuition of the latter, yet is unable to make them supersensuous. The inner adept is ever ready, ever on the alert, and that suffices for our purposes. At moments of rest, then, his faculties are at rest also. When I sit at my meals, or when I am dressing, reading or otherwise occupied I am not thinking even of those near me; and Djual Khool can easily break his nose to blood, by running in the dark against a beam, as he did the other night . . . and I remained placidly ignorant of the fact. *I was not thinking of him*—hence my ignorance. (*The Mahatma Letters* 257)

Being human, the adepts have personalities. When the idea occurred to Koot Hoomi and Morya that it might be useful to bring some of their knowledge into the West, Koot Hoomi decided that it was important for him to go to Europe to get a thorough understanding of the European mind. How was he to teach Europeans if he didn't understand them? Although we have no proof, tradition has it that Koot Hoomi studied at Trinity College in Dublin and also took some courses on the continent. He learned to speak English and French fluently. He was (or is) a skilled correspondent, as his letters show. He appreciated music and the fine arts. He had a loving nature, which clearly comes through in his letters. However, he says precisely what he thinks, and so does Morya. But while Morya is very direct in his criticisms, Koot Hoomi is gentler. Both adepts have exhibited a sense of humor in their letters, but it differs in style, just as their whole personalities differ.

Speaking of Blavatsky, Koot Hoomi once wrote that moments after an avalanche he had just witnessed, he was taking advantage of the stillness when his inner quiet was broken. He wrote:

> I was rudely recalled to my senses. A familiar voice . . . shouted along the currents, "Olcott has raised the very devil again! . . . The Englishmen are going crazy . . . Koot Hoomi, *come quicker* and help me!"—and in her excitement forgot she was speaking English. I must say, that the "Old Lady's" telegrams do strike one like stones from a catapult! (*The Mahatma Letters* 15)

Morya's personality comes out clearly in some of the letters as well. He is extremely strong-willed and direct, but not unkind. Since he did not spend much time in Europe, he was not so familiar with Western ways. While he did occasionally correspond with some Westerners, he did not enjoy corresponding. He wrote letters only when he felt it was his duty to do so.

Morya's sense of humor was sometimes full of irony. On one occasion, responding to a student who thought himself unduly important, he writes:

> Two or three sentences [in your letter] . . . are well calculated to make even an *adept* scratch his head. Especially solemn and mysterious is the one that . . . [refers] to a certain secret society. This news that you belong . . . to another Society . . . in which no one member knows the other . . . filled me with awe and admiration. . . . I confess to my great shame that I know very little of it—probably owing to your usual

precaution.... And since regardless of its *carbonari*-like character, that precludes the possibility of one member knowing any other member, you still seem to know *several* of them who claim to know and hold relations with me—I must naturally infer that you are very high in it—its President perhaps, the "High Venerable Master"? (Jinarajadasa, *Second Series* 142)

Morya used sharp irony to help a student who had fallen victim to pride. What he said was meant to awaken the student, not to hurt him. Sharp words do not necessarily mean lack of love and compassion. Parents often use sharp words to help their children, and adepts often do the same to help their students. Morya ends his letter with a warning, but to assure the student that he cares about him, he signs off "Yours still lovingly."

Now what do these adepts do? Do they sit around on hilltops and meditate? What interests them? In their letters they repeatedly state that their primary interest is in working for humanity as a whole. They do work with certain individuals, but only if the individual can be useful in the work for humanity. Even then, psychic rapport with the individual is far more likely than physical contact. Under no circumstances do they work psychically or physically with individuals for personal reasons.

It is not that the adepts have no friends or do not enjoy some people more than others. They say that until the very end of human evolutionary development, far beyond where they are, one still has personal preferences. But they will not act on such preferences, because if they acted out of personal motives they would entangle themselves once more in personal karma.

Because they are convinced that human beings must learn through their own choices and experience, they never subject anyone to their will. Some people think that the adepts will give us personal advice or even orders. On this subject, Koot Hoomi wrote: "The adepts . . . are forbidden by our wise and intransgressible laws to completely subject to themselves another and a weaker will,—that of free born man" (*The Mahatma Letters* 59). And Morya wrote: "We *advise*—and never *order*. But we *do* influence individuals" (*The Mahatma Letters* 134).

Acknowledging that they do influence people, Koot Hoomi wrote: "At favorable times we let loose elevating influences which strike various persons in various ways. It is the collective aspect of many such thoughts that can give the correct note of action" (Jinarajadasa, *First Series* 99–100).

There is a curious phenomenon that may be the result of their influence. History attests to the fact that occasionally certain scientific discoveries pop up all over the world at the same time. Might it be that the adepts have had something to do with that? Of course, even an adept could not influence a mind that was ill prepared to gain insight. The mind has to be open to an influence, and the intuition has to be reasonably developed. Another example of what may have been partially due to their influence is the democratic movement that sprang up around 1776 and is still spreading. Of course, they would not approve of the violent, fanatical actions often carried out in the name of some noble causes. As they say, people respond to their influences in various ways. The adepts never force.

How do the adepts influence others? One method is certainly by the power of thought. Thought power is not the constant flow of words and images through the mind. That action has some effect because there is nothing in the universe, whether the flapping of a butterfly's wings or a slight feeling of emotion in us, that does not have its effect on the whole. But our constant run of thoughts and feelings has only a negligible effect, much like a tiny pebble dropped into the middle of the Pacific Ocean. Although it eventually affects every atom of that ocean, for all practical purposes such a small disturbance goes unperceived.

Thought power can be described as a utilization of creative energy directed by a centered, one-pointed, and fully focused mind. That kind of power is said to be able to move mountains. We may be doubtful about such power, although experiments have shown that some people possess the ability of psychokinesis; that is, they can move an object by the power of their mind. Such ability is exceedingly rare, and only a few have been shown to possess it.

Theoretically, before anyone can move an object with mind power, he or she must have a clear and unwavering mental focus. Yet few of us can hold our minds on a specific object or thought for more than a few seconds. If you think you can, try to think of a clock for thirty seconds. You will find that in five or ten seconds you are thinking, "Why am I doing this? I wonder if I can move the hands on the clock? I see it is 10:15 a.m." It is not easy to keep the mind one-pointed and focused. It requires an enormous amount of training.

Even if we do not accept that the mind can move objects, consider the power of thought in human society. There is an old saying about an idea whose time has come. When such an idea arrives, it can literally topple empires. Remember what happened to communism in Eastern Europe. It disappeared almost overnight. Its demise was caused by thought, augmented by physical conditions certainly, but thought was really the driving force.

By thought power and other means, the adepts are helping to shape the future. Koot Hoomi made this clear to Sinnett when he wrote:

> A crisis, in a certain sense, is upon us now, and must be met. I might say two crises—one, the Society's, the other for Tibet. For, I may tell you in confidence, that Russia is gradually massing her forces for a future invasion of that country under the pretext of a Chinese war. If she does not succeed it will be due to us; and herein, at least we will deserve your gratitude. You see then, that we have weightier matters than small societies to think about; yet, the T.S. must not be neglected. (*The Mahatma Letters* 15)

Notice the word *if.* The masters do not force or control. They are interested in any movement and any idea that can be useful in the work of furthering the evolution and the development of humanity. Most likely they influence science as a whole and scientists individually, as well as philanthropists, political visionaries, humanitarians, religious leaders, and many others—anyone whose ability, work, and goodwill has equipped them to be of service.

The adepts regard science as one of their most powerful allies. In another letter to Sinnett, they wrote:

> The doctrine we promulgate . . . must . . . become ultimately triumphant as every other truth. Yet it is absolutely necessary to inculcate it gradually, enforcing its

theories . . . with direct . . . evidence furnished by modern exact science. (Jinarajadasa, *First Series* 2)

The adepts reject blind belief of every sort, and it does not matter to them whether or not an individual believes that they exist. Belief in their existence does not flatter them, and lack of belief does not insult them. In either case, they work through the mental atmosphere, lighting up the best path to follow. It is then up to the individual to act. They have done their part; nothing more happens unless we do ours.

Many people think, "If I just believe in the masters, if I am devoted to them, if I meditate on them every day, they'll be interested in me and I can be their student." Belief and devotion will not draw the attention of the adepts. Throwing ourselves wholeheartedly into work for humanity will. We have to *do* something.

The masters say, in fact, that we can "force" an adept to take us on as a student. But "forcing" them means living an altruistic life. For many, this may prove difficult. It is easier to think of the adepts as godlike and expect that if we are reasonably good, they will give us the knowledge and powers we want.

Since the adepts were introduced to the West, many have regarded them as miracle workers or saints, before whom we should prayerfully clasp our hands. Some believe that by just meditating on the masters we will become like them. But if we only do that, we make them objects of worship, and that is something that they emphatically reject.

Although the adepts are far more knowledgeable and developed than most of humanity, they do not think of themselves as superior. If we are the parents of a four-year-old child, we don't think of ourselves as superior to that child. We simply realize that we know much more about the world. It is a little like that with the adepts and us.

In a 1900 letter to Annie Besant, Koot Hoomi noted the tendency for a worshipful attitude toward them and wrote:

> Are we to be propitiated and made idols of [?] . . . Let the devotion and service be to that Supreme Spirit alone of which each one is a part. (Jinarajadasa, *First Series* 99–100)

He also once wrote, "Learn to be loyal to the idea, rather than to my poor self" (*The Mahatma Letters* 432). They prefer that we think of them and ourselves as colleagues. That is a very different attitude from regarding them as saints or gods. Despite the differences in our ability and knowledge, if we want to, we can become their colleagues in the work for humanity.

The more one learns of the adepts, the more natural it is to feel reverence, love, and respect for them. That is appropriate, and perhaps even useful. But what they really want from us is a commitment to work for the good of the human race. That work does not have to be in some momentous, glorious way that the world will acknowledge. Everyone can do something, and we have their word that a watchful attitude for opportunities to do such work brings us into magnetic rapport with them.

The Mahatma Letters are not an organized textbook on Theosophy. They are individual letters, most of which were replies to specific questions from Sinnett. Since we do not have Sinnett's letters, we can only surmise what those questions were from the answers given. Some letters dealt with specific situations at the time. The issues discussed in those letters were important then but not now. Nevertheless, frequently nestled into a discussion of then-current events one finds a gem of truth that sheds light on the human situation today. Other letters are devoted primarily to the philosophical teachings of the adepts. Those letters contain valuable insights into the nature of our universe and indeed of our own human nature.

What of the Theosophical Society that resulted from the teachings of the adepts? The objectives of the Theosophical Society emphasize the unity of the human family; the comparative study of religion, science, and philosophy; and the investigation of human potential and natural laws. If those objectives were carried out extensively, humanity as a whole would be the benefactor. Humanity as a whole, however, can be reached only through individuals. So in addition to carrying out the objectives of the Society, the adepts seem to have something else in mind. They want each member to try to bring Theosophical philosophy to others. Koot Hoomi, quoting an even wiser adept, wrote:

> It is not the individual and determined purpose of attaining oneself Nirvana (the culmination of all knowledge and absolute wisdom) which is after all only an exalted and glorious *selfishness* but the self-sacrificing pursuit of the best means to lead on the right path our neighbor, to cause as many of our fellow-creatures as we possibly can to benefit by it, which constitutes the true theosophist. (Jinarajadasa, *First Series* 3)

Bringing this philosophy to others so they can benefit from it is very different from preaching. When we preach, we want somebody else to believe what we do. That's not what the adepts want. They want us to teach this philosophy to others not only by precept, but by the example of our lives, to quicken others into self-realization for their own benefit and the benefit of humanity. That's what they want. They want us to help free humanity from its misery and misunderstanding. There is a line in the Bible that says, "Give me understanding and I shall keep Thy law" (Ps. 119:34). It is understanding that enables us to act wisely. That is why the Society brings this philosophy to people.

The Theosophical Society has yet another purpose. Its branches serve as a testing ground for members. It is not that some adept is creating a test. Life will do that quite naturally. An adept was once asked why the masters did not intervene in disputes in the Society, and he answered that they will never take charge of the Society's affairs. Besides, when controversy arises, it presents an opportunity to see who stands for principles and who for personalities.

The example of acting for principle rather than personality was well set by the adepts themselves. A. O. Hume was an extremely well-educated but arrogant Englishman who, along with Sinnett, became interested in these teachers. He thought he was greatly superior to the adepts in some ways, but nonetheless he was curious about them. They saw his faults. They took verbal abuse from him, as well as his arrogance and superior attitude. They once said Hume's only interest in humanity was in the first syllable of the word. Yet they worked with him patiently, because he could do something. And he did. He became a leader in the movement to free India from colonial rule, something that the adepts thought necessary.

People often ask if Morya and Koot Hoomi are still living and still inspiring individuals to work for the common good. Since the adepts are not their physical bodies, whether or not they are still living *physically* does not matter. The inner self, the true adept, does live on and the individuality (buddhi-manas, not the personal ego) endures through all incarnations.

Although the adepts seldom work with individuals personally, individuals can still come within the sphere of their influence. Like-minded people are in rapport with one another even if they do not realize it. Whenever individuals aspire to work for the common good, they enter a common stream with everyone who shares that aspiration. That common stream is greatly strengthened by the thought power of the adepts. Therefore, anyone entering that stream is greatly influenced by them. This is all the more true if we think of them, not personally, but impersonally in the sense that we want to be in harmony with and contribute to their work for humanity.

Some people today claim to be in touch with various adepts, including Morya and Koot Hoomi. One need only compare the alleged new messages from the adepts to *The Mahatma Letters* to see that the content and the style of the later messages differ radically from *The Mahatma Letters*. Whatever the source of the published newer messages, it is almost certain that it is not an adept. Often the content of the new messages is personal. Yet the adepts have made it clear that they do not intervene in anyone's personal life.

Thinking of another person has an effect on them. The thoughts reach that person, whoever they might be, adepts included. In 1900 Koot Hoomi was disturbed by the stream of thought reaching him from the idly curious. In a letter to Annie Besant he wrote, "The cant about 'Masters' must be silently but firmly put down. . . . Nameless and silently we work and the continual references to ourselves and the repetition of our names raises up a confused aura that hinders our work" (Jinarajadasa, *First Series* 100). Since about 1960 some organizations have raised that "cant" again, and along with it, the "confused aura" that hinders the impersonal work of the adepts.

Some wonder if the adepts have abandoned the Theosophical Society. In some cases, perhaps that is true. At the same time, whenever they believe that the Society is moving in the right direction, they will energize it with their influence. If the Society and its members are not working to carry out its true purpose, then the adepts will abandon it.

Those who are willing to work for the common good can become distant colleagues of the adepts. If we drop all personal motives and try to discover what is truly right, then we will automatically enter into the stream of the adepts' influence. By entering that stream our own spiritual aspirations will be strengthened and insight into right action may come. Fortified with greater strength and understanding, we can then contribute to their work for humanity by thought and by deed. This may seem wishful thinking to some, but by trying it we may discover that it is true. Whether or not we try is up to us.

Chapter Eleven

WORLDVIEWS AND HOW THEY AFFECT US

In chapter five, we identified the personal ego as an illusion created by habitual patterns of thought and feeling. Those patterns are so strong in us that, along with the body, they become "me." That illusory self overshadows the true self, and in doing so it creates a great deal of our psychological pain.

In this chapter we are going to consider another type of illusion. That illusion is based on the equally strong conviction that our view of the world and its cultures is accurate and ethically right. Although many people are unconscious of it, everyone has a worldview. Whether our worldview comes from a religious or secular perspective, our values are based on what we think is real and what we think is right. This in turn determines our behavior.

Speaking about religion, Mark Twain once said that human beings were the only creatures that had religion, the true religion—several of them. He might just as well have been speaking of our worldviews. We are often convinced that our worldview is the true one. Yet there are more than several "true" ones. If we are ever to come to an accurate view of reality, we must first be willing to consider the fact that at least portions of our worldview may be illusory. The following example may help to make this clear.

If we should be walking along a country lane and come upon a snake, we act immediately. Very few people would think before acting. If we are thoroughly familiar with snakes, we might act in one way. If all we know about snakes is that they could be dangerous, we might act in another way. In either case, our action will be determined by what we think we see, what we know, and our state of mind.

What if unknown to us the object that we see is not a snake, but a rope? On discovery that we had been mistaken, our actions would appear foolish. We might think, "I nearly broke my leg jumping out of the way, and I nearly had a heart attack, all because of a rope in the lane." Our knee-jerk reactions are frequently determined by what we think we see, what we think is real.

The way we live is also based on what we think we see. We base our life, not on what we see physically, but what we see psychologically and spiritually. Whether we know it or not, we live according to a constellation of values and practices that are based upon what we believe to be true about our world.

Obviously, the culture in which we are raised will have a profound influence on our values. If we are born to Buddhist parents, we will likely develop a Buddhist worldview. If we grow up in an atheistic state, such as the former Soviet Union, we may think that religious concepts and values are worthless superstition.

A cultural worldview can be so powerful that in certain cases it contributes to the destruction of a community. A case in point is described by Jared Diamond in his book *Collapse: How Societies Choose to Fail or Succeed.* In that book he describes two early Viking settlements in Greenland. The people who founded those settlements were law-abiding Roman Catholics, and they were an economically stable community. In their Norse homeland they had raised cattle, sheep, and goats. They had also hunted caribou and seal. When about a thousand years ago the Vikings settled the Greenland communities, they treated the land just as they had treated the land in southern Norway. They attempted to provide pastureland for their animals. The forests provided them with wood to build their customary homes. It also gave them firewood to heat those homes. This was the way they lived in Norway. It was part of their cultural identity. The trouble with that was that Greenland was not Norway. The ecosystem was not strong enough to support the lifestyle of the community.

It would have been sensible for the Vikings to reduce their livestock, but owning cows was a mark of high social standing in Norway. Reducing the number of cows ran contrary to their worldview. For the communities to survive they should have adopted some of the Inuit practices. The Inuit used seal blubber, not wood, to heat their homes. They had perfected the art of hunting ringed seals, which were an abundant food source. The Inuit ate fish, but the Vikings would not, because it was a cultural taboo for them to eat fish. The Vikings considered the Inuit to be no more than worthless wretches. To live as the Inuit did would have been to deny their own culture and adopt an inferior one.

Rather than eat fish, they finally ate their own cattle and their pets in order to stay alive.

Diamond suggests that in the end the Viking communities vanished because they refused to adapt themselves to the land. The Inuit had done that, and they survived long after the Viking communities disappeared. The Viking worldview was so powerful that it negated common sense and largely contributed to the demise of the Viking settlements in Greenland.

It should be abundantly clear that two worldviews often collide. Misunderstanding, prejudice, and even wars have resulted from the clash of cultures. How a community sees the world plays a large role in human history.

While religious and cultural teachings are powerful elements in our worldview, they are not the only ones. If they were, everyone born into a particular culture would see the world in exactly the same way. Obviously, they do not. Other equally powerful factors enter into the construction of our worldview.

Our parents and teachers influence us, either positively or negatively. Scientific theories and political ideologies affect us, and the influence of our peers is sometimes overwhelming. The stronger personality, with all of its strengths and weaknesses, often overshadows the weaker personality. This fact is so obvious that parents frequently try to keep their children away from the "wrong" group of friends.

The media are also a powerful source in shaping our worldview. Reporters focus on sensational events. Television newscasts are filled with tragic deaths and the devastation of war. Seldom do we learn of the thousands of acts of kindness experienced daily by people everywhere. The constant bombardment of negative news tends to make us believe that the world is a wicked and cruel place. If that is how we see the world, we may become suspicious of others without reason. In severe cases, we may even become suicidal. No doubt some people are hostile and threatening, but most people are not. If we realize that, our worldview becomes more balanced and accurate, and the way we behave changes in a positive way.

Perhaps more than any other factor, our personal experience shapes the way we see the world. A dog or cat that has been mistreated will often attack without warning, or it will flee from imagined danger. The animal has been conditioned by experience. We are not so different.

If we have had a great deal of tragedy in our lives, or if we have been severely abused, we react like mistreated animals. On the other hand, if we have lived in a relatively harmonious and loving environment, we react more positively to others. Our personal experience has a major impact on the way we perceive the world and on the way we behave.

According to Willis Harman, the late president of the Institute of Noetic Sciences, most people perceive the world in one of three ways. He labeled these as Metaphysic 1, 2, and 3, abbreviated as M1, M2, and M3.

The M1 view is materialistic monism, that is, matter and energy are the only reality. One learns about reality from the measurable world, the world we can detect by our five physical senses. There is no creator, ultimate meaning, or destiny. Morality is subjective and results from biological determinants, personal history, conditioning, or sheer chance.

Those who consciously or unconsciously see the world from the M1 perspective behave differently from those who see the world from the M2 or the M3 perspective. If we believe that the only real world is that of matter and energy, then physical life must be preserved *at all costs.* Even if brain dead, we might want the body to be kept on artificial life support. We would measure success by material wealth, power, and fame. Only what can be measured by physical science is real; all the rest is imaginary. My thoughts and feelings do not affect others unless I tell them how I feel. That is because my thoughts and feelings are going on inside my physical body and could not possibly affect others at a distance.

The M2 view is Cartesian dualism. There is a dichotomy between mind and matter. Perhaps the mind, or the soul, survives physical death, but mind is more likely a product of the brain and dies with it. In any event, the world of the mind, or soul, and the physical world are separate.

Those who subscribe to this view tend to compartmentalize their lives into physical and spiritual sections. If the world of the mind and the physical world are separate, then the laws of the one may not apply to the other. We may therefore find a person who is a physicist but who also belongs to a religious cult. That person believes that the spiritual world is a *different* world, and that the laws of physics do not apply in the spiritual domain.

The M3 view is transcendental monism. Consciousness, not matter, is primary. Reality is contacted through consciousness. Rather than being a by-product of matter, consciousness transcends matter.

Individuals who hold this view may be deeply spiritual or religious. What is most important to them is the condition of their soul, or consciousness. Meditation and prayer may be an important part of their lives. Material wealth may be useful, but it is not the most important thing in life.

We may not realize that we have a worldview, but by examining our behavior it becomes obvious that we do. Someone once said, "What you are speaks so loudly that I can't hear a word you are saying." The way we live reveals our true worldview. We may have convinced others and ourselves that we see the world from a spiritual perspective and that we identify with our inner self rather than with the body. Then we are told that we have a terminal disease. If we truly identify with the inner spiritual self, we would continue to live life to the fullest in the time we have left. If subconsciously we really identify with the body, we panic. We may become severely depressed or go into denial, pretending that we are not ill at all. Our true values determine our behavior even if we are self-deceived.

Even science and medicine are affected by the predominant worldview of their cultural context. Many years ago Dr. J. B. Rhine of Duke University dared to suggest that the university set up experiments to determine whether or not some individuals possessed extrasensory perception. He did not say he wanted to prove that they did; he merely said he wanted to get to the bottom of the question by scientifically examining the issues. Dr. Rhine's colleagues were appalled. They found it outrageous that he would even suggest that their respectable university examine "superstitious nonsense." Dr. Rhine nearly lost his job because the predominant worldview of the time was materialistic monism, or at best, Cartesian dualism. Although parapsychology is still not regarded as legitimate science in many quarters, some universities now have departments for the study of extrasensory experiences.

Until recently, doctors thought that psychological factors were unrelated to physical problems. Drugs and surgery could cure anything that was curable. That belief was consistent with the Cartesian dualistic worldview. Today the psychosomatic factor is widely recognized by the medical profession. Aspects of the medical worldview are changing.

Our worldview sets up our values, and we act accordingly. Inevitably, our actions produce results, and the results teach us whether or not we got it right. This is true for cultures and it is true for individuals. The materialistic worldview has proven inadequate. Physics has identified nonmaterial fields, doctors have discovered that attitudes of mind affect the body, and some even believe that meditation and prayer have been proven useful in healing. Today one of the approved therapies for cancer patients is meditation. Not many years ago the medical profession would have considered that to be something that only a quack would prescribe.

Although experience may show us what is wrong, it does not necessarily provide us with the correct solution. We must figure that out for ourselves, with or without suggestions from others. Sometimes our experiences convince us that our basic assumptions about the world are untrue. Sometimes we stubbornly retain our belief system even though we are not getting the anticipated results of our actions. In the latter case, we might modify our behavior without changing our basic point of view.

For example, a mother or father may be convinced that the parent knows what is best for the child. While that may sometimes be true, it is not always so. It is particularly unlikely to be true when the child is forty years old. Yet there are parents who still think they know what is best for their forty-year-old son or daughter. Being convinced of that, they try to manipulate their adult child into doing what they want. Perhaps the parent believes that the daughter should get married and have children. Perhaps the daughter has other plans. The parent has discovered that simply begging the daughter to get married provokes an angry response that threatens their good relationship. Ah, thinks the parent, I know that my daughter should find a husband, but she is resisting what is good for her. How can I change her? Perhaps I can make her feel guilty by saying that I wish I had grandchildren. Acting this way, the parent has simply changed behavior in order to achieve the desired result. On the other hand, negative feedback from the daughter may convince the parent that the daughter must decide what is right for herself. In that case, the parent's own worldview has changed.

While we may all agree about what is in principle good and what is not, we do not prioritize our values the same way. Individual life experience causes us to value some qualities over others and to detest some qualities more than others.

It is relatively easy to see how our cultural worldview affects us. It is not so easy to see how our individual worldview affects us. Yet if we really want to understand our selves and the world, then it is essential that we discover how our personal worldview masks reality.

Some years ago a major corporation provided supervisory employees with an educational program designed to help them deal more effectively with their subordinates. One session in the program was designed to show the supervisors that they were subject to bias. Usually when we think of bias, we think of racial or ethnic bias. The object of this training session was not to discover racial or ethnic bias, but unconscious bias towards certain character traits in people. The exercise chosen for the training session proved to be quite effective. Many supervisors were shocked to discover bias that they did not realize they had. In one case a supervisor realized that she tended to ignore employees who expressed themselves loudly. The exercise did not specifically identify that bias, but it did encourage participants to search for any bias they might have. Many discovered biases that blocked their effectiveness on the job and their relationships with people in general. Whether or not we can get along with people often depends in part on elements of our worldview, elements such as unconscious bias.

If you would like to discover why you and your friends react differently to certain types of people, then you might want to read the following hypothetical tale and ask yourself a few questions about the characters in it. If you ask a few friends to do the same, you may be surprised by the results. The purpose of the exercise is to show how some unconscious values affect our behavior toward others.

Annabelle Lee is a young woman who lives in lower Alabama. She lives on one side of a river and her fiancé, Michael, lives on the opposite side. The river is called Gator River because there are many alligators in it. Annabelle Lee and Michael have selected their wedding date and have invited all of their friends to the wedding, which is to take place on Michael's side of the river.

The night before the wedding, there is a fierce storm that destroys the only bridge across the river. Since Annabelle Lee does not have a boat, she realizes that she cannot get across the river without help. Immediately she remembers that Sam the fisherman lives just a bit downstream. She runs the short distance to his home and asks him to take her across on his boat. Sam replies that he cannot do so because his nets were severely damaged by the storm and he must fix them. "After all," he says, "the income that I get from fishing is essential to my family and me."

Finding herself defeated, Annabelle Lee returns to her home, sits on the riverbank, and begins to cry. Soon she sees a boat coming toward her, and she attracts the attention of Sinbad the sailor. She asks if he would take her across the river so that she might be married as planned. Sinbad declares that he will do that, but that she must do something for him. He says that if she will give herself to him for just half an hour, he will take her to the other side of the river. She is shocked, but she decides that there is no other way to get across, so she agrees. Having achieved what he wanted, Sinbad then fulfills his promise by depositing her on the other side of the river, and he wishes her a happy wedding.

Now on the opposite side of the river she runs to Michael's home, knocks on the door, and waits expectantly for Michael to answer. When Michael opens the door he is shocked to see her and asks how she got across the river. Annabelle Lee tells him the whole story, including the bit about Sinbad. On hearing that, Michael says that he could never marry a woman who had done such a thing, and he shuts the door in her face.

Annabelle Lee is now on the opposite side of the river crying. Shortly the last character in our story, Sluggo, appears. "What's wrong?" he asks. Annabelle Lee tells him the whole story, including the fact that Michael now refuses to marry her. Sluggo is infuriated. He goes to Michael's home, pounds on the door, and when Michael answers, he knocks him out cold. This ends the tale.

Answer the following two questions based *only* on the information you have been given. Do not add or subtract anything. Please answer them with your first reaction. Do not analyze the characters. There are absolutely no right or wrong choices. Here are the questions:

1. Which character in the story do you admire most? Even if you think they are all rather reprehensible, choose the one you think is the *least* reprehensible. Now write down what it is about the character that caused you to make your selection.

2. Which character in the story do you find most reprehensible? Now write down what it is about the character that caused you to make your selection.

You may rank all the characters by selecting the second best or the second worst, etc.

When this story is told in large workshops, someone votes each character best, and someone votes each character the worst. Occasionally husbands and wives vote differently, much to the amusement of all.

Many say that Annabelle Lee was the best because she was resourceful, honest, and loving. Others see her as the worst because she was willful, lacking patience, and determined to get her own way at any cost.

A few say that Michael kept to his principles, and they admire that. Others say that Michael was prudish, intolerant, and unforgiving. Today, Michael does not get many positive votes. Fifty years ago, however, he would likely have had a large number in his corner. Times and cultural worldviews have changed.

Sam put duty to family first, but some people point out that Sam was unwilling to help a person in need, even when it would not have taken him much time to help.

Sinbad was definitely an opportunist, but he was also honest and he kept his word.

Sluggo had a strong sense of justice and wanted to defend those whom he believed had been unfairly hurt. However, he heard only one side of the story and he reacted with violence.

Our personal life experience tends to affect the way we react to people, even hypothetical ones. Those who dislike Sam are sometimes people who have been in charge of getting volunteers for nonprofit organizations. They have heard so many excuses for not helping that they react negatively to Sam because he would not help, even though the amount of time involved could not have noticeably reduced his income. Those who like Sam believe that responsibility to family and work should come first. Consciously or unconsciously, they subscribe to the Protestant work ethic.

While Sinbad does not get many positive votes, those who deal with labor negotiations sometimes vote him best. That is because they want to know what each side is really willing to accept and they want each side to be honest and to keep their word. Sinbad did that.

In one workshop, an older couple was so strongly opposed to sexual relations before marriage that they thought Michael was completely virtuous. When his negative qualities were identified, they were surprised. They had not noticed them. Conversely, some people are so opposed to opportunism that they fail to see that Sinbad had some virtuous qualities. The way we choose our best and worst character has a lot to do with how our individual experience has molded aspects of our worldview.

Most people regard the Gator River story as an amusing tale that stimulates animated discussion about the faults and strengths of the imaginary characters. A few people find it shocking and distasteful. Occasionally one or two people refuse to judge the hypothetical characters at all. In each case, our response to the story is determined by our values. What we think is important and unimportant, right and wrong, all derive from our own worldview. That strongly influences our response to the story and its characters.

Perhaps no two people will ever see the world in exactly the same way because no two people share the same experiences. Scientific discoveries, changing social conditions, psychological insights, and personal experience all contribute to our understanding of the world and our selves. All of that changes over time, and that changes us and the way we see the world.

In order to fully live a spiritual life, it is essential to rid ourselves of the illusions ingrained in the subconscious. The exercise just described may help us to realize that we sometimes admire or condemn others based solely on one single quality that we either admire or despise. We do not see the *whole* person. Consciously or unconsciously, we are condemning the "sinner" rather than the "sin." Judging others in that way blocks spiritual growth. If we see that in ourselves we might change for the better.

We have considered several worldviews, their values, and the behavior that derives from those worldviews. We may now consider the Theosophical worldview with its values and behavior.

The Theosophical worldview is based on the three fundamental propositions (or principles) of *The Secret Doctrine*. As we have seen, the first of these posits an underlying unity behind all phenomena, the second declares that everything in the universe is subject to cyclic law, and the third affirms that the universe gradually unfolds or evolves.

Those who have a worldview based on these principles are likely to behave quite differently from those who reject such a view.

If we are convinced that at the most profound level of our being we are one with all that lives, then we are likely to have reverence for all life. Harming others, ravaging nature for personal gain, and the like would become unthinkable.

If we realize that cyclic law (orderly change) is a universal reality, then we will know that everything changes. Poetically speaking, we will know that we can never stand in the same stream twice. If we do not realize that, we are apt to create unfortunate and painful experiences for ourselves by trying to stop the stream. There is even a key to successful relationships in this principle. Those who expect that their relationships will always remain the same become disillusioned when they do change. And they will change. It is nature's law.

If we accept the Theosophical view of evolution, we will realize that within us there is a vast potential to be actualized. We will make every effort to dig within ourselves to find previously unknown resources to be used in solving the challenges of life.

The values and the life that follow from these fundamental principles can be summed up this way:

The Theosophical Society, while reserving for each member full freedom to interpret those teachings known as Theosophy, is dedicated to preserving and realizing the ageless wisdom, which embodies both a worldview and a vision of human self-transformation.

This tradition is founded upon certain fundamental propositions:

The universe and all that exists within it are one interrelated and interdependent whole.

Every existent being—from atom to galaxy—is rooted in the same universal, life-creating Reality. This Reality is all-pervasive, but it can never be summed up in its parts, since it transcends all its expressions. It reveals itself in the purposeful, ordered, and meaningful processes of nature as well as in the deepest recesses of the mind and spirit.

Recognition of the unique value of every living being expresses itself in reverence for life, compassion for all, sympathy with the need of all individuals to find truth for themselves, and respect for all religious traditions. The ways in which these ideals become realities in individual life are both the privileged choice and the responsible act of every human being.

Central to the concerns of Theosophy is the desire to promote understanding and brotherhood among people of all races, nationalities, philosophies, and religions. Therefore, all people, whatever their race, creed, sex, caste, or color, are invited to participate equally in the life and work of the Society. The Theosophical Society imposes no dogmas, but points toward the source of unity beyond all differences. Devotion to truth, love for all living beings, and commitment to a life of active altruism are the marks of the true Theosophist.

Chapter Twelve

THE PATH

In the spiritual traditions of the world, ritual, prayer, meditation, almsgiving, and similar activities are often thought to be essential elements of the spiritual path. While the rituals differ widely from faith to faith, all traditions require a simple and ethical life. Each tradition warns against selfishness and pride. Each tradition requires a reverence for life. To many, the mere outward observance of the rules assures them that they are on the spiritual path. They believe that if they follow all the rules, they will get to heaven or to whatever reward is promised them.

Most of us have probably seen a young child pretending to be an adult. A young girl might wear her mother's high-heeled shoes or put on some lipstick. A young boy might carry his father's briefcase or toolbox around the house. The adults know that high-heeled shoes and briefcases do not make a mature person, and usually we smile at the child who is pretending to be an adult. We know that one does not become an adult by taking on certain outward symbols. Gradually our way of life changes. We are no longer interested in the toys that were once so important. When we reach adulthood, we are wiser, or at least more knowledgeable. We do not *make* ourselves into adults; we *become* adults.

Antonio Machado, a Spanish poet, wrote, "*Caminante no hay camino. Se hace camino al andar.*" "Traveler, there is no road. The road is made by traveling." This simple, poetic statement is close to the Theosophical view of the spiritual life. We cannot achieve spiritual enlightenment by following rules. This is why the Theosophical Society does not have a set of commandments or even a prescribed practice that members are required to follow. We cannot achieve enlightenment by artificially imposing a lifestyle upon ourselves. There are altruistic spiritual giants who are vegetarians. At the same time, there are intensely selfish people who are vegetarians. If we become vegetarians because we think we will gain some spiritual power, we have become vegetarians for selfish gain. If, on the other hand, we have a deep sense of unity with all that lives, then the resulting compassion may lead to a vegetarian lifestyle. This is not to say that all spiritual people are vegetarians. Blavatsky was a deeply spiritual woman. She recommended a vegetarian diet, but she was not a vegetarian herself.

All agree that in order to live the spiritual life, one must be an ethical person. But who is to say what is ethical? While we may all agree that it is wrong to indiscriminately kill our fellow human beings, we do not all agree that it is wrong to execute criminals. When it comes to sexual conduct, there is even more disagreement. The Roman Catholic Church forbids the use of any kind of artificial birth control. Other religious groups believe in family planning that includes the use of birth control. What is declared to be ethical differs from group to group and from person to person.

Most people think that ethics are rules of conduct that tend to be written into law. Some believe that a god presented them in the form of commandments. Others see ethics as merely a sensible way of conducting oneself in society. The Theosophical view is quite different. Rather than arbitrary laws set down by a god or a secular government, ethics are seen to arise out of the very fabric of nature itself.

The common definition of "nature" is the countryside of trees, rivers, and mountains. Of course that is nature, but from a Theosophical perspective, only an outer form of it. Nature is that eternal Reality that is the very ground of all that is, subjectively and objectively, spiritually and physically. Nature is the order that pervades the universe in all its aspects. It is "absolute, immutable law" revealed in an ever-changing world and all its creatures.

Since perpetual motion is one of the laws of nature, everything is always changing. Therefore, we cannot set up a rigid list of rules for ethical behavior. What is right for the seed is not right for the plant. Behavior that is right for the two-year-old is not what is right for the forty-year-old. If we are to live truly ethical lives, we must discover how the eternal principles operate in nature and in ourselves. If we understand nature's laws and cooperate with them, we may learn how to free ourselves and the planet from pain and suffering. Indeed, men got to the moon because our scientists understood the law of gravity and cooperated with it. As Jesus said, it is the truth that sets us free.

Shorn of a simplistic understanding, karma is the fundamental law of nature. Every action, at whatever level, produces a reaction. Every cause produces an effect, both physically and psychologically. This simple, universal fact has been discovered in some form or another in science, psychology, sociology, religion, and philosophy. We may not always be able to connect cause with effect, but we can be fairly certain that there is a cause behind everything that we experience.

If we are careful observers, we may learn from every experience. That is true collectively and individually. Those in authority may teach us an ethical system, but it is our experience that validates or invalidates the teaching. We learn from the consequences of our actions. We learn from experience.

What we do depends largely on who and what we think we are. If we identify with the body, then we do what the body wants. We may ignore the alarm clock in the morning because we are enjoying a delicious sleep. We sleep on for several hours, then get up and eventually show up late for work. Our physical action has psychological effects as well as physical ones. Those who sleep in too often are likely to lose their jobs.

Many identify primarily with their emotions. We may be enjoying a late-night party to the extent that we ignore the needs of the body. By 2 a.m. the body is desperately in need of sleep, but we (or rather, our emotions) want to keep enjoying the party. We refuse to go home and get to bed. The consequences of such action, especially if frequently repeated, may affect us for days or even affect our health much later in life.

Those who identify with the mind may find themselves in an even more dangerous snare. Fanatics of every description are convinced that they *know* the truth. They are so identified with their beliefs that they may be willing to kill or die for what they believe. If we are offended or upset when others disagree with us, we can be certain that we have identified with the mind.

Those who have discovered the spiritual within themselves, and who have begun to identify with it, act differently. Because they have sensed an essential unity with humanity, they tend to act for the good of the whole. They do not neglect their own real needs, but they are careful not to act for personal gain at the cost of harm to others.

Just as children eventually tire of their toys, we adults tire of ours. Having identified with the body and our personality throughout life, and perhaps through many lives, we have acted from that personal center and reaped the results of our actions. Sooner or later, we tire of the whole process, and we long to understand the meaning and purpose of our life. Then, like the ignorant Fool on the Tarot card, we set out on our quest, determined to find ourselves and our place in the scheme of things.

Chapter Thirteen

THE DIRECTION

Standing at the threshold of a new life, we are perplexed. We do not know where to go or what to do. We want to find someone who knows the way, someone who has achieved the victory, someone who can lead us. We want that person to tell us what to do.

Siddhartha Gautama, the Buddha, was similarly perplexed when he set out from the luxury of his palace to discover the cause and cure for suffering. He began by turning to the ascetics who claimed that they knew the way. Experience taught him that they did not. He searched on, and we are told that by his own effort he became enlightened. He taught that without relying on authority of any kind, we should seek our own salvation with diligence. He knew that the teacher can only point the way, because the way is our individual life. To awaken the divine reality within ourselves requires a way of life that is not based on arbitrary rules but on understanding and action.

The great spiritual teachers have always taught that there is but one direction that leads toward salvation. It is from the fleeting to the everlasting, from the changing to the eternal, from the personal to the universal. It is a way of self-sacrifice fraught with hardship and danger, but at the same time it is a route to reward past all telling. Legend and myth have spoken of it. The great mythological figures frequently must pass through terrible trials without any guarantee of success. These figures represent every person who ventures on the great journey of self-transformation and self-discovery. As there are riddles and paradoxes to solve in some legends, so there are riddles and paradoxes to solve on this new journey. Jesus taught that if we try to save our life, we will lose it. If we lose our life for his sake, we will gain eternal life. Just as mythological men had to solve riddles, we must solve that one. It is not an easy task, but the possibility of success makes it worth all the effort it may take to solve it.

Blavatsky gave us some guidelines for living the spiritual life. These are contained in a short statement that she said came from a letter written by one of the adepts. It is known as the "Golden Stairs." It reads:

A clean life, an open mind, a pure heart, an eager intellect, an unveiled spiritual perception, a brotherliness for one's co-disciple, a readiness to give and receive advice and instruction, a loyal sense of duty to the Teacher, a willing obedience to the behests of Truth, once we have placed our confidence in, and believe that Teacher to be in possession of it; a courageous endurance of personal injustice, a brave declaration of principles, a valiant defense of those who are unjustly attacked, and a constant eye to the ideal of human progression and perfection which the Secret Science depicts. These are the golden stairs up the steps of which the learner may climb to the Temple of Divine Wisdom. (*Collected Writings* 12:503)

We are asked to try to live in accordance with those guidelines, but we are not given a foolproof method or a promise of success. If the yearning for union with the infinite is strong enough in us, we will persevere to the end. We will fail many times, but so long as the inner light does not go out, we will try again and again until success comes.

The Golden Stairs describe a perfected state that we may try to realize. It is a state of complete wholeness and integrity. Jesus said, "Be ye therefore perfect, even as your Father which is in heaven is perfect" (Matt. 5:48). Unfortunately, the word *perfect* is used mostly to mean without any error or blemish. Since we and our whole world are conditioned states of the eternal, that kind of perfection is impossible. What the admonition intends to say is that we should be complete, whole. We can strive toward wholeness, and the Golden Stairs can point the way to success.

In one sense the stairs are sequential, and in another they are not. For example, without a pure heart, we might not be motivated to live a clean life, and without an eye to the ideal of human perfection we might see no point in trying to climb the other steps.

As we progress, our understanding of what each step represents will change. Each one has depths of meaning and many applications in life. We might make a start by considering each step individually as we see it now.

A clean life is required by all the major religious traditions and by good people everywhere. We understand that a clean life is an ethical life. Yet our understanding of what is

ethical may change over time. At first it may be seen in negative terms, that is, what we should *not* do. That may
broaden to what we *should* do, and then become what is
truly right to do. In addition, a clean life may imply something so simple as keeping the physical body clean. That
may extend to eating only wholesome food, neither too little nor too much. We may realize that alcoholic drinks,
drugs, and even junk food may be "unclean" in the sense
that they are harmful to the body. Since we are more than
the body, we might also seek to maintain clean emotions
and a clean mind. A clean mind requires more than the
absence of unpleasant thoughts. It requires cleanliness in
the sense of clarity. It requires a mind that is free of prejudice, free of set ideas. Since we are all conditioned by our
experience and by our culture, we tend to see and judge
everything and everyone through the conditioned state of
our mind. We may be free of racial prejudice and yet be
totally unaware that we are prejudiced against ideas that contradict our own point of view. A clean life is the first step on
the Golden Stairs, but it is filled with depths of meaning.

There are those who believe they have an open mind
because they simply don't have any strong convictions of
their own. They listen to whoever speaks the loudest and
believe them until someone louder comes along. Rather
than open minds, they have empty heads. Such people are
rudderless boats, swept away by the strongest current and
frequently shipwrecked by a storm.

Others believe that they have open minds because they
are willing to listen to all sorts of new and fascinating ideas.
Should one of those ideas go against their own, however,
they will reject the new idea as being unworthy of consid-
eration. Truly open-minded people are willing to consider

any evidence that points toward truth. They will drop their own most precious ideas in a flash when confronted with strong evidence that these are false. Open-minded people are not interested in defending their own opinions; they are open to any idea that may lead to truth.

When we try to justify our own opinions, we are motivated by self-interest. We want to be proven right. We want to triumph over the other person. Our motive is not pure. Selfless motive may be what is meant by a pure heart. Unfortunately, the word *heart* is often used to mean the emotions. In Buddhism the heart is thought to be the seat of wisdom, not emotion. If the heart is pure, the motives are pure. If we use the mind to devise clever arguments in order to justify our views, we are not seeking truth, and we do not have a pure heart. We have a heart stained by selfishness.

Without a reasonably clean life, open mind, and pure heart, we could create a nightmare for ourselves and for the world by using what we have learned for selfish purposes. The intellect that is let loose within an unclean life, a closed mind, and an impure heart can bring and has brought about enormous suffering. One need only look at history and at current affairs to see that this is true. Selfishness armed with powerful intellect is a grave danger. In *The Voice of the Silence* we read, "But even ignorance is better than Head-learning with no Soul-wisdom to illuminate and guide it" (25). When the life is clean, the mind open, and the heart pure, the intellect can be safely directed. Blavatsky tells us that "there is no danger that strong intellect cannot surmount" (*Collected Writings* 13:219). Without the prerequisites, an eager intellect could create danger rather than surmount it.

If we expect to come to wisdom, it is not enough to have an open mind and a pure heart. We need an eager intellect that will search for truth wherever it may be found. If we only have an open mind and a pure heart, we may be like the Fool on the Tarot card. He may have an open mind and a pure heart, but because he is not actively using his intellect, he is oblivious to the danger before him.

The first four steps of the Golden Stairs may bring us closer to an unveiled spiritual perception that pierces through the illusion of separateness. We become more and more aware of our unity with humanity as a whole. By no means have we achieved enlightenment, but we have realized that all men are our brothers and all women our sisters. We might then ask, "Who is my co-disciple?" and the answer may be that everyone is our co-disciple. We are all learning from our experience, and we can all learn something from every person we meet.

Brotherly feeling for one's co-disciple does not require us to feel personal affection for everyone. That is impossible. What we can do is realize that each one of us must face, and hopefully conquer, many difficulties in life. On the surface we are unique. Yet, arising out of the same ultimately indivisible Reality, we are one at the source of our being. From a sense of unity at that profound level we can send goodwill even to those for whom we feel no personal affection. Without that deep sense of unity, our actions may be far from brotherly.

Just as there will always be those who know more than us, so will there always be those who know less. Rightly understood, "a readiness to give and receive advice and instruction" is a sensible attitude of mind. There are many people who are always ready to give advice but seldom willing to receive it. Conversely, there are many who think that they are unable to give advice to others. Both are mistaken. Each one of us can learn from someone wiser than we are, and we can help those less wise by teaching them what we have learned.

Telling people what to do is not what is meant by a readiness to give advice. When a person asks for advice, they are usually faced with a difficult choice and find themselves unable to decide what to do. We might think that a particular course of action is best for them, but if we try to convince them to accept our decision, we are imposing our will onto theirs. Except in the case of small children, that is seldom wise. On the other hand, if we suggest various courses of action and allow them to make their own decisions, they may suddenly realize what is right for them. That may be the best advice of all.

There are both ethical and unethical spiritual teachers. There are also those who truly know and those who are self-deceived. The unethical ones know very little and charge a great deal. The ethical ones may not charge, but if they are self-deceived, their information is often both useless and harmful. It is up to us to discern the difference.

In the Golden Stairs, the word *Teacher* is capitalized. There may be a clue in that simple fact. Who is the Teacher? Is it necessarily another person or an adept? More likely, the true Teacher is the inner self, that most profound reality within each one of us that is Truth itself. In *The Voice of the Silence* we are told to seek in the impersonal for the eternal self: "Look inward. Thou art Buddha" (26).

If we are to obey "the behests of Truth," we first need to open our minds to insight from that enduring self that is at one, not only with the adepts, but also with Truth itself.

Since self-deception is a constant danger, we must be on guard against believing that our opinions are direct revelations of truth. A valid insight into Truth brings with it a peace that passes understanding and an inner certainty that is unshakable. It is a reflection of the Eternal, and it is what is meant by true faith. Faith has nothing to do with opinion or blind belief, and it is never accompanied by the emotional violence of anger that we so often hurl against those who disagree with us. True faith is not blind belief. In the words of the New Testament, it is "the *evidence* of things unseen" (Heb. 11:1).

The Buddha asked that we accept only what appeals to our common sense and reason. That is good advice, no matter whether the Teacher is an adept or our own inner self. Certainly we should not put our trust in anyone or any supposed insight from within ourselves if it violates common sense and reason. That which is beyond the rational mind's ability to picture does not violate reason. We may, for example, entertain the concept of infinity without being able to picture it or even prove it. That does not violate common sense or reason. On the other hand, if we are told to go to a mountaintop on a specified date because alien spaceships are going to carry us to heaven on that day, that does violate common sense and reason.

Common sense dictates that when attacked, we are right to defend ourselves. Why, then, are we required to have "a courageous endurance of personal injustice"? This is all the more perplexing when we find that the very next step requires "a brave declaration of principles." Taken together, these two steps may be better understood.

Plato tells us that Socrates was condemned to death for teaching a doctrine that was contrary to the established one.

Rather than recant what he knew to be true, he accepted the judgment of the court. It so happened that while in prison Socrates had a chance to escape because some of his wealthy friends had bribed the guards. Socrates refused the offer. His students were astounded. Why, they asked, would he not take his freedom and live? Socrates replied that he would rather die than give up philosophy. Also, he felt bound to the city by a social contract and would not break that bond. Rather than accept freedom, he bravely declared his principles and courageously endured personal injustice.

We are now asked to valiantly defend "those who are unjustly attacked." The operative word in the sentence is "defend." When someone whom we admire is criticized, we may get angry and attack the critic. This is frequently disastrous because when people are attacked they often dig their heels in and defend themselves. They assert their case even more strongly and stop listening to the one who is attacking them. On the other hand, if in defending the unjustly accused we remain calm and state the facts as we know them, there is a chance that the defense will be heard and even considered.

In the end, if we are not convinced that we can further develop our human potential, we should not try to climb the stairs that lead to the Temple of Divine Wisdom.

The Golden Stairs give us a clear view of what is required to reach the Temple of Divine Wisdom. They state the goals, but they do not tell us how to go about climbing that metaphorical stairway. Since the method must vary from person to person, no single method is valid for all. Yet the goal is the same for all. Because of that the Theosophical Society does not prescribe a method for spiritual development. At the same time, the Society offers the Golden Stairs as guidelines to all who aspire to tread the spiritual path to the final goal.

In addition to the Golden Stairs, Theosophical tradition has long held that there are three limbs of the spiritual life. They are study, meditation, and service. We are not told how or what to study, or how to meditate, or how to serve. We are only told that study, meditation, and service are central to the spiritual life. Rightly understood and practiced, study, meditation, and service help us to climb the Golden Stairs to the Temple of Divine Wisdom.

Chapter Fourteen

STUDY

Clearly all knowledge is useful, but some is more useful. Whatever we learn may be used to benefit others and ourselves. What we choose to study depends on what motivates us to study. If we are driven by personal desire, we may gain a great deal of knowledge, but it will not move us one inch on the spiritual path. If we are driven by a thirst for ultimate truth and a longing to help bring our fellow human beings to that truth, then we are motivated rightly. By using our power of discernment, we will choose the areas of study that will most effectively lead to that noble goal. We may choose to study the spiritual literature from the saints of humanity. We may even put to good use what we learn from studying mechanics, computer programming, science, history, art, and a host of other things.

Many people believe that study requires a great deal of reading and research. Reading and research are an important part of study, but taken alone they are not really study. We can easily read something, believe it, remember it, and convince ourselves that we have understood what we have read. Remembering is but a study tool that is sometimes useful and that sometimes blocks understanding. When it comes to comprehending universal principles, reading and remembering are not enough. If understanding were simply a matter of remembering, then a DVD could be an enlightened being. Understanding a principle always comes as a flash of insight. We suddenly *get it*. In a timeless moment, all the pieces come together in our mind and we realize that we have discovered an unshakable truth.

If we expect to digest our food properly, we must not gulp it down without chewing it. Seldom do people stop to realize that intellectual food should be treated in the same way. Some people are intellectual gluttons. They devour book after book, cram their heads with facts of every description, and make themselves sick from mental indigestion. It is far better to read a little and think a lot. We need not do this with mystery or romance novels, but we do need to do it with any serious work.

The Theosophical Society does not offer a required course of study, partly because the Theosophical view is that while we are all fundamentally one, each person is unique. We learn in our own way and at our own pace. Having said that, there are major Theosophical works that are worth serious study. Among these are *At the Feet of the Master, The Key to Theosophy, The Secret Doctrine, The Mahatma Letters, The Voice of the Silence,* and *Light on the Path* (see suggested readings). A lifetime of study would not be sufficient to glean all the gems from these works.

The Theosophical Society does not tell its members what they should study or how they should study. Yet there are hints in the literature pointing to a method that we might call Theosophical. This is a contemplative or meditative approach to study that may enable the student to go beyond mere intellectual comprehension.

Using this meditative approach, we may come upon an idea that intrigues us but that we do not fully comprehend. Rather than racing ahead to acquire more ideas, we might pause to reflect on the one that interests us but at the same time escapes us. By pondering for a bit, off and on, for days or even for weeks, we may suddenly get a flash of understanding. By pondering, we have been stimulating the intuition, that aspect of our nature from which insight and understanding spring. Only when our mind becomes one with a truth do we understand it. Studying in this way is a kind of meditation. The intellect has been fed a thought, but it then rests quietly while we seek deeper within for the insight that will bring understanding. The flash of understanding comes from buddhi, the principle within us that enables us to know a truth because it is Truth itself. The intellect is a tool that enables us to acquire factual knowledge, but, working alone, it does not bring understanding. If we use only the intellect and do not invoke insight, we may wind up knowing everything and understanding nothing.

Contemplative study is a kind of meditation that dwells on the subject at hand. We are pondering an idea or theory that has been put before us. We are seeking to understand. Meditation proper often brings understanding and insight into a principle, but that is not its primary goal. Just as happiness results from doing what we love to do, understanding and insight follow from true meditation.

Chapter Fifteen

MEDITATION

It has been clinically proven that those who meditate feel more energized and less anxious. In fact, meditation is now taught to patients in many hospitals around the world. Yet meditation is far more than a stress-reduction technique. It can harmonize the whole person, balance moods, and sharpen the mind. More importantly, if we long for union with the Infinite, meditation is capable of awakening the inner self.

Many people find that it is easier to meditate in a group than to meditate alone. That is because we are all interconnected and we affect one another. If there are experienced meditators in a group, they will stimulate others in the group by radiating peaceful energy during the meditation. Without group support, it requires a greater effort to get started and to deepen meditation. Even so, in the long run, it is important to learn how to do it on our own. When we do that, we can go much deeper and achieve even more than we could at first in a group meditation.

There are many methods of meditation, and there are many practices that are incorrectly called meditation. Some are useful, some not, and some are even harmful. While prominent members of the Theosophical Society have recommended various forms of meditation, Theosophists are free to choose any method that they find useful. Therefore, while we may say that there are Buddhist or Christian forms of meditation, we cannot say that there is a "Theosophical" meditation. Some Theosophists choose not to meditate at all; others choose a meditation from a religious tradition or one that they have devised themselves.

Theosophical lore has it that Blavatsky was once asked, "What is the most important aspect of the spiritual life?" She replied, "Common sense." She was then asked, "What is the second most important aspect of the spiritual life?" She replied, "A sense of humor." It should be easy to see that humor is based on what is incongruous, and in order to see what is incongruous, we must know what is congruous. People with common sense know the difference between the two. Finally, Blavatsky was asked, "What is the third most important aspect of the spiritual life?" Her swift reply was, "More common sense." In meditation, as in everything else, common sense may keep us from harmful practices.

Healing meditations for others and oneself are among the most popular and useful types of meditation. Their results are so convincing that meditation is now one of the therapies used in cancer treatment. Creative visualization is a common technique in healing meditations. In one such approach, patients are asked to daily visualize white blood cells consuming and destroying cancer cells. Statistical evidence suggests that patients who do this have a better chance of conquering the cancer, or at least living longer than the control group.

A few researchers claim that prayer and meditation for people at a distance have been proven helpful. One's religion does not seem to matter. What matters is that when we think of a person who is ill, and we sincerely want what is best for them, we are likely to have some effect on them. There is some evidence that even if we do not know the person for whom we meditate, our thoughts do affect them.

Some years ago a woman who played the organ for Sunday morning Mass was looking for an assistant. A friend suggested a Juilliard student who might enjoy playing every other week, or at least once a month. The friend said that she would pass on the name and phone number of the organist who wanted help. Several months passed without word from the prospective assistant. Then one night at dinner with her husband the woman said, "I wonder if that woman is ever going to call about playing the organ?" The remark was a total *non sequitur*. Within a minute, the phone rang. The woman's husband answered, and a confused voice on the other end asked, "Is there a Mary Morrisson there?"

Neither woman had ever met the other, and because a man had answered, the caller was not even sure that she had the right number. In this case, it would seem, the thought of one person did affect the other person.

There are many examples of thought affecting others at a distance, some examples even coming out of university experiments. If we can reach one another by thought like that, it is reasonable to suppose that we can send healing energy to someone else by the power of thought. Using the same principle, we can send peaceful thoughts and love to individuals, communities, and the world. The Buddhist meditation of lovingkindness is an example of this type of meditation. The steps in that meditation are roughly as follows:

> May I be well, peaceful and happy.
> May my family and friends be well, peaceful, and happy.
> May everyone in my city be well, peaceful, and happy.
> May everyone in my country be well, peaceful, and happy.
> May all beings in the world be well, peaceful, and happy.

The meditation then goes in reverse, from all beings, to the country, city, family, friends, and self. Merely saying the words is useless. We might think the word *peace* for hours and do no good at all if it is merely a word. We might just as well think *ginger ale*. The word is only useful if it prompts the actual power of peace within us. If it does that, then by an act of will we can project that peace outward to the world.

Among the potentially harmful types of meditation are meditations on specific chakras, or energy centers of the body. Practiced by proficient, knowledgeable meditators, such meditations may have their place. Among novices, focusing on chakras will probably do more harm than good. In one extreme case, a woman regularly focused on the brow chakra, commonly called the third eye. Perhaps she thought she could awaken psychic powers. In any case, after some time she developed severe headaches. Nevertheless, she would not stop the practice. The daily intense routine so affected her that eventually her eyes were visibly bulging from her head.

Some meditate in order to awaken what they believe to be the kundalini energy. Kundalini is said to be a transformative energy that is concentrated in the chakra at the base of the spine. Theoretically, it is dormant in most people, but active in highly evolved, spiritual people. When awakened prematurely, it may cause serious physical and psychological difficulties. Just as it is best to let puberty develop naturally, so it is best to let kundalini develop naturally. Forcing either could do serious damage. Fortunately, most people who believe that they have awakened this energy are self-deceived. In order to awaken kundalini one needs to have a strong, focused intellect and an intensity of purpose.

In one case, a young man in his thirties did manage to awaken the kundalini energy. He reported that his spine became intensely hot and that his emotions became so powerful that they were completely beyond his control. He spent weeks in the hospital, terrified. He wanted to know how he could stop it and never have it affect him again. The man was intellectually brilliant, and he was one who did nothing by half. He was also an extremely intense individual. Had he not been, it is unlikely that he would have been able to do what he did. Unfortunately, having lost touch with the young man, we do not know whether he was able to reverse the damage and live normally thereafter.

Of course there are many types of meditation designed for specific purposes. If compassion is what motivates us to meditate, we have made a good start in any type of meditation. So long as what we are doing is peaceful and harmonious, our meditation will likely be helpful. If it produces headaches, psychological upset, or frightening experiences, we are doing something wrong. In this case it is wise to stop immediately.

Proper meditation will never be upsetting. On the contrary, it is refreshing, energizing, and integrative. Some people who teach meditation say that the practice will evoke dark, negative feelings that must be processed. To put it this way is extremely misleading. What meditation is likely to do is first to get us more in touch with the inner self, which is always peaceful. Meditating on the inner self will never bring negative feelings. However, by trying to awaken the inner self, we are delving deep within ourselves, through and beyond the psyche. That practice brings to the surface our inner potential both for good and for ill. It does not do so during the meditation, but the consequence of meditation in our everyday life is to become more aware of our whole nature, both the good and the bad. After practicing meditation for some time, we may discover that we have awakened abilities that we did not know we had. We may also discover that we have a dark side to our nature, and that we must overcome it. That is not the same thing as evoking dark and negative feelings during a meditation. If dark and negative feelings surface during meditation, we have not identified with the inner self at all, but rather with the dark side of our own psyche. By awakening the inner self, we may eventually see the dark side of our nature, but also see what it is that we must do to neutralize it.

Speaking of the first aspect of meditation, clearing the mind, *The Voice of the Silence* tells us that "mind is like a mirror; it gathers dust while it reflects. It needs the gentle breezes of Soul-Wisdom to brush away the dust of our illusions. Seek O Beginner, to blend thy Mind and Soul" (26).

The dust is the residue of thoughts along with the images and memories that have accumulated in the mind over time. Whenever the mind is not actively engaged in some task or focused on solving a problem, uninvited thoughts arise spontaneously. When the mind relaxes, thoughts rush in. They are almost always personal thoughts, the things that have happened during the day, the plans for later that day or in the future, and especially the things that have caused us anxiety. Soon we find that our stream of consciousness has carried us far away from the present moment and our surroundings. We are not in control of our mind or thoughts. Our mind and thoughts are controlling us.

If we simply say, "I can't do anything about it," then we will not try to gain mastery over the mind. On the other hand, if we are willing to admit that it may be possible to gain such mastery, then we may begin the process. Remembering that inertia is a mental and emotional principle as well as a physical one, we will accept the fact that years of mental inertia cannot be totally changed by one meditation session. It will take time, effort, and practice to train the mind in a new way.

Often we are told that we must learn to concentrate before we can learn to meditate. Concentration is essential to meditation, but it need not be mastered before we begin to meditate. The object of our concentration and meditation has a great deal to do with the likelihood of success. If we choose to concentrate on a matchbox, for example, it is almost inevitable that our mind will wander within a few seconds of our attempt to concentrate. We have no real interest in a matchbox. If we choose an object associated with strong emotion and thoughts, such as a favorite childhood toy, we'll almost certainly get lost in associated thoughts and feelings.

An excellent choice for beginning a meditation session is a tree, a mountain, or a waterfall. Almost everyone has experienced a sense of peace at some time when they were in nature. Trees and mountains do not feel human anxiety, and almost everyone who really looks at them feels a bit more peaceful and refreshed by the experience. Unfortunately, most people only perceive them; they do not *see* them.

If you are motivated to learn to meditate, select a place in your home where you will meditate for a short period every day. Ideally, the room should be lighted, but not too brightly. It is often best to practice in the morning, simply because what we do early in the day tends to set the tone for the day as a whole. Sit comfortably in a chair or on the floor with spine erect and legs uncrossed, or in the lotus position if you know how to take that position and feel comfortable with it.

If you happen to find that you can meditate more easily in the evening, that is acceptable. However, it is best not to meditate in complete darkness or only by moonlight. Theoretically, one may be more susceptible to negative forces in complete darkness or moonlight. While that may not be true, it is best to avoid the possibility.

To begin, take a few deep breaths and relax. Then make a conscious intent that whatever you are able to achieve in the meditation will affect you during the day, or the next day if you meditate before going to bed.

Now think of something in nature that has given you a sense of peace. It may be a distant scene or a favorite tree in your own yard. Without being fussy about getting the image just right, visualize the tree briefly and try to feel at one with it. Most likely, you will begin to feel a bit more peaceful. Feel the peace pour through you, even through to your feet. After a few minutes make an effort to radiate that peace out to the world. If you are a novice, it is wise to do this exercise for only a few minutes, not more than five. That is simply because your mind may not be used to focusing on one image for very long. In time, you may lengthen the session by a few more minutes.

Having made the intention to have your meditation be effective during the day, you are likely to find that if you begin to feel tense or anxious the image of the tree will return to your mind. Take a deep breath and think of the tree again for a few seconds. This will not solve the problem before you, but it will relax your mind again and help to make it easier to decide what to do. This simple meditative exercise can help to quiet the mind and begin to sweep out the dust of thought. It is only a beginning, but it is an important and useful beginning.

After days, weeks, or even months of daily short meditations to clear the mind and feel peace, you may be ready to deepen your meditation.

Perhaps all valid meditations have a tendency to activate the inner self. There are, however, practices that lead more directly to this awakening. In such meditations, as with all meditation, the preliminary work is to clear the mind of thought. As you may already have discovered, that is no simple task. Yet by short, regular practice, we can learn to do that. Having achieved clarity of mind as best we can, we may now begin to seek out the impersonal self within and realize that we are that self. As with anything worthwhile in life, this kind of meditation takes effort. It is, however, an *effortless* effort, achieved without stress or strain of body or psyche. Effortless effort is not associated with our emotional feelings or desires. Rather than effort, we might say that it is a strong, one-pointed intention to discover the inner self by letting go of the *personal* self. Effortless effort relaxes us but keeps the mind alert while it seeks its own source.

When you are ready to go deeper, begin with the meditation on nature and send peace as usual. Next, try to find a center of absolute stillness within. It may be helpful to center consciousness at about the level of the heart, but not in the physical heart itself. It is the center of your being, rather than a physical organ. The stillness that you may eventually discover there is not the stillness of the graveyard. It is a point in the Eternal, and you *are* that point. Nothing can harm you in that stillness. There you are totally nonreactive. You observe whatever thought that may intrude, but you neither follow it nor judge it. It may be a lofty thought, a mundane one, or a base one. It is a thought, and you simply recognize it as such and allow it to die without reacting to it or following it. For as long as you reasonably can, keep your mind focused on the stillness that you are. Try to realize that in that state there is no time, no "me," but only eternity.

While you are identified with the inner stillness, you may do a healing meditation for someone in need. You can do far more good from this profound level than would ever be possible from the emotional level alone. It is best to select only a few people to think about during each meditation session, perhaps not more than three. While universal healing energy may be unlimited, our ability to focus it and send it *is* limited. It is not necessary to visualize the person in need, although you may do so if you wish. Think of the person as whole. Do not think of the illness itself. Simply send the energy to them, trusting that it will help them either physically or just psychologically. We do not know what is best for another person. Sometimes it is right for them to die. In that case, the meditation will not cure their bodies, but it may well bring them peace and acceptance of death.

Whether or not you do a healing meditation, it is good to end each meditation session by radiating the inner peace throughout your own being, even through to your feet. Then send that peace and healing out to the world once more.

Almost everyone who meditates notices some positive effects from the practice. At first it may only be that you feel a bit more calm and peaceful. There may be nothing more than that for months or even longer. Meditation tends to reach a plateau and remain there for some time. However, if you persist in trying to deepen the meditative experience in each session, you will one day suddenly become aware of a more profound state of consciousness within you. That will also plateau. New depths may follow new depths to no conceivable end, each one occurring in a flash that is akin to a new birth.

The benefits of daily meditation can hardly be exaggerated. Regular meditation changes us. The way we react to problems will change. Whereas in the past we might sometimes have panicked, we now find that we can remain still within ourselves and more effectively meet challenges. Insight comes more frequently, not only so-called spiritual insight, but insight into solving daily problems. We are likely to become more compassionate. We are more apt to be calm, even when others are upset. Meditation will not make us saints, nor will it prevent challenges. It will, however, better equip us to handle the challenges that come to us. Meditation is an essential element of the spiritual life.

If you truly long for union with the Eternal, you are rightly motivated. Armed with that and a never failing determination to awaken the inner, immortal self, you will eventually succeed. Once that self is glimpsed it cannot be forgotten. Yet even that is not the final goal. Of this, Blavatsky writes:

> In his hours of silent meditation the student will find that there is one space of silence within him where he can find refuge from thoughts and desires, from the turmoil of the senses and the delusions of the mind. By sinking his consciousness deep into his heart he can reach this place—at first only when he is alone in silence and darkness. But when the need for the silence has grown great enough, he will turn to seek it even in the midst of the struggle with self, and he will find it. Only he must not let go of his outer self, or his body; he must learn to retire into this citadel when the battle grows fierce, but to do so without losing sight of the battle; without allowing himself to fancy that by so doing he has won the victory. That victory is won only when all is silence without as within the inner citadel. (*Collected Writings* 8:127–28)

Ultimately meditation is much more than regular practice sessions. It is an integrative process. Over time, the inner self, the mind, the emotions, and the body become harmonized with one another. More and more, our life is directed from within the stillness that we are. If we demand instant success, we will fail. If we persevere to the end, we will achieve. The rewards are worth all the effort we could possibly make. As Blavatsky says:

> If . . . man looked . . . *within himself* and centered his point of observation on the *inner* [self], he would soon escape from the coils of the great serpent of illusion. From the cradle to the grave, his life would then become supportable and worth living, even in its worst phases. (*Collected Writings* 8:116)

Surely every human heart longs for that. The cost in effort and persistence is enormous, but to live a life that is "worth living, even in its worst phases" justifies it all.

Chapter Sixteen

SERVICE

All the great religious traditions teach that service is an integral aspect of the spiritual life. We can contribute service to charitable organizations, hospitals, schools, and religious organizations. All of that may be useful and deeply appreciated by those who need our help. Yet from a Theosophical point of view, it may or may not be true service. To repeat what one of the adepts said in a letter, "motive is everything for us" (*The Mahatma Letters* 295).

There are many who serve because they believe they are expected to. Some do it to be seen and praised by others. There are corporations that expect their employees to do some charitable work so that the company wins the admiration and therefore the business of its clients. Employees who serve in order to get high marks on their evaluations are not really serving, no matter how much good their work may bring about.

Sometimes when people think that they *should* serve, they become meddlesome. We cannot remove all of the world's ills single-handedly. We must learn to see what we can do and what we cannot do. Sentimentality often interferes with real service. When we cannot help, it is essential to accept that fact. If we become sentimental and try to help when we cannot, we may make matters worse and waste time trying to do the impossible when we could use that time to do what we can do.

What we do in order to serve is not nearly so important as the attitude of mind that prompts us to serve. From a Theosophical point of view, true service is a way of life that results from an interior state. The insights that we gain through study and meditation become part of our very nature. They change us. We become more conscious of a deep unity with all that lives, and compassion naturally flows out of that realization. When we see someone in need, and we know that we can help, we do. We do it not because we have been taught to be charitable, but because we cannot do otherwise. It is part of our nature. We cannot walk away from serving because we cannot violate our own nature.

A true story may help to illustrate the nature of real service. Many years ago there was an old lady who played the organ for a small church in New York. She worked as a nurse on a night shift in a Queens hospital until she was in her eighties. When she got off work on Sunday morning she would travel to Manhattan, arriving at about 8:30 a.m. She would have breakfast and then go to the church, prepared to play for the service at 11:00 a.m. At 12:30 p.m. she would have lunch with members of the congregation and then travel to her sister's home in Queens for a few hours of sleep, after which she returned to the hospital for work.

Members of the church were amazed by the strength of her dedication. One Sunday at lunch people around the table were praising her. She could not understand why they were going on about it. She was rather annoyed by all the praise, and she ended it with one statement. She said, "Please stop it. I'm just doing what I want to do." The woman served because it was her nature. It was not work to her. It was a joy.

To live a life of service means that when we see something that we can do to help a fellow human being, an animal, or a plant we do it instinctively. We need not donate many hours to charitable work. The simple act of smiling at a supermarket clerk who seems unhappy is service. If we see a broken bottle on the sidewalk and remove it so that no one will be hurt by it, we are serving. Whenever we act selflessly to do what we can to bring joy and harmony into the life of a fellow being, human or other, we are serving. Those who render true service do so because it is part of their nature. They can do no other.

Study, meditation, and service are one whole. Study is a kind of meditation, just as meditation is a kind of study. Service is the inevitable result of true study and meditation, because these two lead to a realization of the ultimate unity of all life. Compassion flows from that sense of unity, and compassion is made visible by the action of service.

Chapter Seventeen

THE STEEP AND THORNY ROAD

The *Voice of the Silence* is an extraordinary guidepost for living a life that is said to lead one ultimately to enlightenment. The book is not for everyone. In fact, Blavatsky dedicated it "to the few." Reading only the first few verses of the book reveals why only a small number of people would take it seriously.

The preliminary verses tell us that we must become indifferent to the objects of perception and seek out that which produces thought. This is no simple task. The vast majority of the human race would probably have no interest in becoming "indifferent to the objects of perception" and would reject the idea immediately. Few would have any interest in trying it, especially when they realize the hardships, dangers, and self-sacrifice required to reach the goal set before us.

In the short piece entitled, "There Is a Road," Blavatsky mentions a secret gateway. "There Is a Road" is not included in *The Voice of the Silence*, but both point in the same direction. While *The Voice of the Silence* describes the steps along the path, "There Is a Road" simply points toward that path and assures us that although it is steep and thorny, we can with effort reach the goal. This little piece highlights both the hardships and the possibility of overcoming them. It reads:

There *is* a road, steep and thorny, beset with perils of every kind, but yet a road. And it leads to the very heart of the Universe.

I can tell you how to find those who will show you the secret gateway that opens inwardly only, and closes fast behind the neophyte forevermore.

There is no danger that dauntless courage cannot conquer.

There is no trial that spotless purity cannot pass through.

There is no difficulty that strong intellect cannot surmount.

For those who win onward, there is reward past all telling: the power to bless and to save humanity. For those who fail, there are other lives in which success may come. (*Collected Writings* 13:219)

Throughout the spiritual literature of the world, a road, path, or journey has often been used as a metaphor for a way of life. Just as a physical road is useless unless traveled, so is the metaphorical way of life useless unless lived. In *The Voice of the Silence* we read: "Thou canst not travel on the Path before thou hast become that Path itself" (12). There is no actual path or road apart from our own evolving self. There is only a way of living, and the experiences that change us.

In one sense there are only two roads. The one that most of us choose is the sensate one. This is the road that winds through feelings of every description. Our experience on this road tells us that we *are* our feelings. This road is not wrong. We learn as we travel it, but we learn ever so slowly over many lives.

The other road is often portrayed in myths and legends as one that is traversed in danger. Yet the reward at the end is worth all the trials that the journey requires. Where is that road? Why is it so perilous, and why is the gateway to it secret?

This less-traveled road is the one whose gate opens "inwardly only and closes fast behind the neophyte forevermore." It opens inwardly to our thoughts, feelings, desires, hopes, aspirations, and ideals. It also opens to a reality beyond all that, beyond the "me" with which we identify. It opens to who and what we truly are.

If the gate that opens inwardly is simply a gate to the self with which we are familiar, it certainly does not close fast behind us forevermore. There is hardly anyone whose personal nature has not been modified to some extent over years. Sometimes our experience changes us. Sometimes we make major changes through psychotherapy. As we grow older, friends often notice that we have grown more mellow. The familiar self can be modified. The gate to that self does not close fast forevermore. We can go in and out, modifying the "me" or not as we please or as circumstances force us to change. Moreover, there is nothing secret about that kind of gate.

The gate that closes permanently behind us is not a gate to self-analysis. It is not a gate to new ideas or theories about ourselves and the world, not even Theosophical theories. Rather, it is a gate that opens to a totally new state of consciousness, to the first experience of the inner self. This experience is qualitatively different from the everyday experience of "me." It is an impersonal state in which there is no longer a sense of self and other, no longer duality, but only the Eternal. So long as we identify with some state within us and say, "This is I," there is the duality of subject and object. There is the self that observes and the object, or state of consciousness, that is observed. In *The Voice of the Silence* we read:

> When waxing stronger, thy Soul glides forth from her secure retreat: and breaking loose from the protecting shrine, extends her silver thread and rushes onward: when beholding her image on the waves of Space she whispers, "This is I,"—declare, O Disciple, that thy soul is caught in the webs of delusion. (4)

Why should the road to self-discovery be fraught with danger? Perhaps it is because every major transition stage in life brings with it the possibility of a psychological breakdown. Passing through puberty, marriage, and the death of loved ones are all transition points. In each case we might say that the old self must die to allow the new self to be born. In the case of passing from the personal self to the inner self, we must face and conquer our psychological furies. We must consciously kill off the old self in order to allow the new self to come into being. That can be a painful process. As St. Augustine put it, "There is no greater sorrow than being no longer the old Adam, but not yet the new Christ." If we rephrase it as "no longer the old child, but not yet the new adult," every teenager will be able to relate to that statement.

Although we are bound to meet our dangerous psychological demons on the road to self-discovery, we can conquer them if, in spite of all failures, we continue to try. Every success brings us closer to the ultimate goal, and every failure reveals one more dead end in the maze we are traveling.

The gateway that leads to the experience of the inner self is secret because it is totally unknown until experienced. Until then, we have only theories about it—words, concepts, ideas, and creeds.

When that inner self is experienced, when for a fleeting forever we *are* that self, there is no time. There is no self. There is only Eternity. Once this reality flashes upon our mind, the gateway closes fast forevermore, because no matter how difficult life may become in the future, we can never forget that at the depth of our being we are rooted in the Eternal.

It is said that when we are born we see a flash of the life to come. In a fleeting instant we understand what it is that we must try to do in that lifetime. The flash is but a preview of our goal. It is not the goal itself. A lifetime of pleasure and pain, joy and sorrow, and challenges of every sort lies before us. Just as that flash preview comes at the beginning of a life, so does the flash awakening of the inner self come at the beginning of a new kind of life. At that moment we have no more reached the goal than the infant has done in the flash preview of the life about to be lived.

At this point, we have yet not reached "the very heart of the universe." We have merely seen that ahead of us lies a steep and thorny road. Only gradually, through challenging experiences, do we discover just how steep and thorny that road is.

One of the first things we may notice on the road is that throughout life we have been automatically reacting to circumstances that come before us. Like a cat that hisses at someone who has abused it, we "hiss" at certain people who have annoyed us. We react emotionally to ideas that threaten our views. If someone upsets us, we remember it. When we meet again, the memory of the upset comes into our mind and we react to it. We do not really see the person as they are *now*. They may have been unaware that they upset us, or they may have totally forgotten the incident that upset us. Instead of seeing the person as he or she actually is, we see our memory of the incident and react to it.

Up to now the mind and emotions have been running us, although we may have been totally unaware of it. While the inner self sleeps, it can do nothing. For us it does not exist. We are only aware of our mental and emotional states and our often feeble attempts to change them. Simply working on ourselves from within the "me" is much like rearranging the furniture in our home. We may make things more attractive by doing that, but it is still the same old house and the same old furniture.

Once the inner self is awakened, we realize that it is from here that we must gain mastery over our whole nature. From here we must rein in the mind, purify it, sharpen it, direct it in ways that are totally new to it, and make it so crystal clear that it will carry out the will of the inner self.

This is a gigantic task. Why? Because our habitual way of thinking and acting has built up a powerful momentum that can only be changed with great effort over time. Commenting on self-purification, Koot Hoomi explained to Sinnett that it is not the work of a moment, but the work of a series of lives. Alluding to psychological inertia, he adds that we must "undo the effects of a long number of years spent in objects diametrically opposed to the real goal" (Jinarajadasa, *First Series* 26).

If we are among the few who long for union with the Eternal, what must we do to obtain it? Blavatsky tells us to begin by becoming aware that we are ignorant of our true nature, and we are constantly self-deceived. Next, she says, we need a deep conviction that with effort we can obtain intuitive and certain knowledge. Third, she adds, we must have an "indomitable determination" to get that knowledge and face it. Such knowledge is unobtainable by rational thought alone. It is the awakening of the divine nature within.

The determination that Blavatsky mentions is the driving force that keeps us on the road to knowledge. If the inner will is weak, if we give up when the road becomes steep and thorny, truth and self-knowledge will elude us.

Armed with an indomitable determination to see ourselves as we are, faults and all, we can begin the long and arduous journey of self-transformation. Unfortunately, there are no clear and detailed maps. On the contrary, there are only guideposts that point toward the ultimate goal. No detailed map will do, because although the goal is the same for all, the route is unique to each traveler. The route is our life.

THE PORTALS

J ust as the outer evolutionary process proceeds by orderly, definable stages, so does the inner side of evolution in human consciousness. Most human beings travel the broad road that winds ever so slowly around the mountain toward its summit. A few take a more direct and arduous route, sometimes referred to as "the Path." They take this difficult route, not out of desire for personal benefit, but from a one-pointed yearning to serve suffering humanity more effectively. Each step on this Path is marked by a major shift in consciousness—a kind of new birth.

This more difficult route has been called by various names in different mystical traditions. In China it is the Tao; in Hinduism, the Path of Initiation; in Buddhism, the Noble Eightfold Path; in Judaism, the Way of Holiness; in Christianity, the Way of the Cross. Plato pointed toward it in his famous allegory of the cave. In this story, the people were all chained to the floor facing a wall on which shadows were cast. Never having known anything else, they were convinced that the shadows were the real world. One day a man freed himself, turned around, and detected a light from above entering the cave. He began to climb the steep walls of the cave toward the light, and in doing so he frequently cut himself on the sharp rocks. Only with great effort did he make his painful ascent to the surface. Seeing the sun for the first time, he was blinded by it. Gradually regaining his sight, he realized that the sun was the source of the light and that the "real world" he had known was only shadows.

All sources indicate that the steep Path is difficult and dangerous but that, if successfully followed, it brings rewards past telling.

To enter the Path one must be consumed by what Blavatsky calls "an inexpressible longing for the Infinite." In biblical terms, one must "love the Lord thy God with all thy heart, and with all thy soul, and with all thy strength, and with all thy mind; and thy neighbor as thyself" (Luke 10:27). Furthermore, the pilgrims who choose to travel that Path must be willing to face the dangers and hardships of the way ahead, and be willing to lose life (that is, the personal ego) in order to find it (the inner self) in Life Eternal.

When we first aspire to follow the spiritual Path, we still think that we are the personal ego. Believing that, we try to improve the ego. We want it (the "me") to become more spiritual. What we do not realize is the fact that the personal ego is very much like a caterpillar. Deep within the caterpillar lies the potential for a butterfly, but that butterfly is liberated only when the caterpillar is dissolved within a chrysalis. The caterpillar is not destined to become a bigger and better caterpillar. It is destined to die to give birth to the butterfly. Efforts to improve the personal ego are laudable; they may even be inspired by the inner self. Yet in the end, the destiny of the personal ego is dissolution. Just as the caterpillar is a necessary stage on the way to the butterfly, so the personal ego is a necessary stage on the way to liberating the inner self. But when the time is right, the personal ego must be dissolved in order for the inner self to be freed.

In *The Voice of the Silence*, Blavatsky says that there are seven steps along the more difficult route. She calls them portals, gates, or paths. She links them to the *paramitas* (measured steps) of the Buddhists. Usually, the term *paramitas* is translated as "cardinal virtues" or "perfections." In Buddhism they are six or ten in number, but while Blavatsky was aware of the six and ten, she lists seven portals. She writes:

> The Paramita heights are crossed by a still steeper path. Thou hast to fight thy way through portals seven, seven strongholds held by cruel crafty Powers— passions incarnate. (46)

The cardinal virtues are translated in various ways. In *The Voice of the Silence* (47–48), they are listed as:

1. *Dana*: Charity and love immortal.
2. *Shila*: Harmony in word and act.
3. *Kshanti*: Patience.
4. *Virag*: Indifference to pleasure and pain.
5. *Virya*: Dauntless energy that fights its way to the supernal Truth.
6. *Dhyana*: Meditation, or ceaseless contemplation of the eternal.
7. *Prajna*: Intuitive understanding or insight. Blavatsky claims that the key to this turns a human being into a god.

It would appear that as each of these virtues is perfected, the opposite vice has to be destroyed beyond resurrection. Every step along the Path leads to a closer union with the eternal self. Every step lessens the hold of the sensate world on the disciple. The personal ego diminishes as the eternal self comes closer to awakening. At every step along the way, the "passions incarnate" of the personal ego resist and the mind attempts to deceive.

Before they have been totally eradicated and replaced by the opposite virtues, the passions may suddenly rise up stronger than before and block every effort the inner self makes to influence us. We may be thrown back to the beginning of the Path and be forced to start the ascent again.

While the various steps along the Path have been described as the perfection of virtues, they may also be seen as major shifts in consciousness, or what some of the literature has called "initiations." It is not difficult to imagine that when a virtue has been fully developed and its opposite vice conquered, the result would be a new state of consciousness or a new birth.

One might say that identification with the sensate personal ego is the root of all vices. Each conquered vice weakens the personal ego as it strengthens the inner self. At the prospect of its demise, the personal ego becomes frightened, tries to deceive us, and urges us to give up the fight to awaken the divinity within, the inner self. As each step on the Path brings the inner self closer to full consciousness, the personal ego tries harder to delay the inevitable triumph. The battles become more fierce, the risk of failure greater, but the victories become more rewarding.

Nearly all traditions report that that in order to become one with the eternal, we must purify ourselves. Because purgation may be difficult and even painful, many have believed that they could be purified by inflicting pain on themselves. Some medieval monks would wear hair shirts, and some Hindus would recline on a bed of nails. Even today some believe that rigorous self-denial will make them spiritual. All this is a distortion of the principle behind self-purification.

The difficulty and pain associated with self-purification are side effects of the process. What is required is that we purify our mind and emotions, not only of vice and selfishness, but also of the constant swirl of disordered thoughts and feelings. The process of purifying the mind of those "impurities" is difficult. It involves the gradual killing off of the personal ego, and that can be a painful process. Only when the whole psyche is free from the impurities just mentioned will it be possible to realize unity with the inner self. Paradoxically, it is the inner self that is behind the purification process. It is the inner self that pressures us to change, even though we may be unaware of it.

While total control of the psyche, total elimination of the vices, and the perfection of all virtues may be far off for most of us, we can begin the work now by seeing and destroying habit patterns that are inimical to the development of the inner self. These habit patterns are not simply physical ones such as smoking or drinking. In fact, the more insidious ones are those that take refuge in the subconscious levels of our emotions and mind. They are the countless ways in which we automatically react to circumstances and people. When we say, "Don't push my buttons," we are admitting that if certain subjects are mentioned, we will become angry. Why? Is it not because we have built up a strong habit pattern of responding in the same way to the same stimulus? Surely that puts us on the level of Pavlov's dogs. We have conditioned ourselves to respond in a particular way. We no longer think. We react without thinking. But with effort, we can identify and overcome our conditioned responses. That is an important step on the spiritual Path.

Theosophical sources tell us that entering the Path in earnest draws down upon us the karma of more than one lifetime. It concentrates the work and speeds up the process. It forces us to destroy vices by perfecting virtues. Challenges that would ordinarily be spread over several lives are concentrated into one. Depending on the intensity and sincerity of our commitment, we are forced to confront and overcome many more difficult problems than we would ordinarily face. This intense acceleration of our karmic debt is what makes the Path, as mystical Christians call it, the Way of the Cross.

Speaking of this Path, one of Blavatsky's teachers wrote:

> You were told, however, that the path to Occult Sciences has to be trodden laboriously and crossed at the danger of life; that every new step in it leading to the final goal is surrounded by pitfalls and cruel thorns; that the pilgrim who ventures upon it is made first to confront and *conquer* the thousand and one furies who keep watch over its adamantine gates and entrance — furies called Doubt, Skepticism, Scorn, Ridicule, Envy and finally Temptation — especially the latter; and that he who would see *beyond* had to first destroy this living wall; that he must be possessed of a heart and soul clad in steel, and of an iron, never-failing determination and yet be meek and gentle,

humble and have shut out from his heart every human passion that leads to evil. Are you all this? (*The Mahatma Letters* 422)

Surprisingly, the very first steps on the Path do not seem so difficult. Rather, they tend to be joyous. One feels born into a new and higher life. In Christianity this stage is symbolized by the Nativity—a joyous time. Speaking of this first stage, Blavatsky writes: "The road that leads therethrough is straight and smooth and green. 'Tis like a sunny glade in the dark forest depths" (*The Voice of the Silence* 52).

The second portal is also somewhat joyous, but omens of difficulty appear. In Christianity it is symbolized by the Baptism. In the Christian story, Jesus is now an adult and he must surely know that although he is beginning his mission, his life will not be easy. About this portal, Blavatsky writes:

And to the second gate the way is verdant too. But it is steep and winds up hill; yea, to its rocky top. Grey mists will overhang its rough and stony height, and all be dark beyond. As on he goes, the song of hope soundeth more feeble in the pilgrim's heart. The thrill of doubt is now upon him; his step less steady grows. (*Voice* 52–53)

The third gate reveals the full extent of the future sacrifice. It is symbolized by the Transfiguration in Christianity. At this point Jesus tells his disciples that he will be taken from them and killed. He now fully knows his destiny. Symbolically, it is the personal ego that must die so that the divine inner self may rise from the dead. Blavatsky writes:

CHAPTER EIGHTEEN

The more thou dost advance, the more thy feet pitfalls
will meet. The path that leadeth on is lighted by one
fire—the light of daring, burning in the heart. The
more one dares, the more he shall obtain. The more he
fears, the more that light shall pale—and that alone
can guide. For as the lingering sunbeam, that on the
top of some tall mountain shines, is followed by black
night when out it fades, so is heart-light. When out it
goes, a dark and threatening shade will fall from thine
own heart upon the path, and root thy feet in terror to
the spot. (*Voice* 54)

The fourth gate is symbolized in Christianity as the
Crucifixion. Blavatsky writes:

On Path fourth, the lightest breeze of passion or desire
will stir the steady light upon the pure white walls of
Soul. The smallest wave of longing or regret for Maya's
gifts illusive, along Antaskarana—the path that lies
between thy Spirit and thy self, the highway of sensations, the rude arousers of Ahankara [egoism]—a
thought as fleeting as the lightning flash will make thee
thy three prizes forfeit—the prizes thou hast won. For
know, that the ETERNAL knows no change. (*Voice* 56)

We may correlate the fifth stage to resurrection. In
one view, stages four and five are aspects of the same experience. That is, every death brings a new birth. The two
go together, the fifth being a natural consequence of the
fourth.

From the very first step on the spiritual path the personal ego has been dying. Each step strengthens the inner

self as it weakens the ego. At this fourth step, however, we must truly lose our life in order to find it. That is, we must let go of the last thread that binds us to the personal ego. Looking back "with a thought as fleeting as the lightning flash" will throw us off balance. This has been symbolized in the biblical story of Lot's wife turning into a pillar of salt because she looked back to the "sinful" city, the world of the personal ego.

Even though the fourth and fifth gates may be lifetimes away for us, we can know something of them by analogous experiences. Everyone goes through little deaths and resurrections in life. The old child dies to give birth to the teenager. The teenager dies to give birth to the adult, and so on. Every day the past dies to give birth to the present. When we cling to and identify with the past, we are identifying with the old self. It is only when the last thread is broken, when the personal ego dies, that the divine inner self can be born. Each little death and resurrection brings new insight and new joy.

The sixth and seventh portals lead on to enlightenment. Intellectually, we may understand enlightenment to be the final insight that brings total understanding of self and the universe in all its aspects. Until experienced, that must remain no more than theory for us.

We may ask, with the poet Christina Rossetti, "Does the road wind uphill all the way?" The answer comes, "Yes, to the very end . . . my friend." We can make it to the end if we do not give up along the way. If we fail the first time that we try, we can try again and again until success comes.

Yet even if we shun the difficult path and take the longer, more common route of collective evolution, it is helpful to remember that often the things that we think are important are, from the view of the inner self, completely unimportant. Whenever we are upset, we can be certain that we have identified with the sensate. By learning to see that our problems are temporal and not so important as we think, we are gradually loosening our bonds to the sensate self.

The next time you get very upset over something, you might remember the little boy who would not eat his prunes at dinner. His mother told him that he had been very naughty. "People are starving in the world," she told him, "and you won't eat your prunes. God will punish you for this." Then she sent him to his room for the rest of the evening. About an hour later a terrible thunderstorm came, and she remembered what she had said to her young son. She ran upstairs to his room to comfort him. When she opened the door, she found him standing with his hands on his hips, looking out at the storm and saying, "Such a fuss for two prunes." Could it be that, however gigantic our problems seem, most of them amount to little more than two prunes?

As near-death experiences suggest, what is finally important is what we learn, how much we grow in strength, insight, compassion, wisdom, and self-mastery. Few other things matter much, and most things don't matter at all. They are just two prunes.

In Mozart's opera *The Magic Flute*, Prince Tamino searches for the beautiful Princess Pamina, who he is told has been kidnapped. He must pass through trials of silence, fire, and water to get to her, but he never waivers in his effort. With his eye fixed on the goal, the prince is not concerned with small matters. He takes the noble path filled with danger. His bird-catching friend, Papageno, takes the more common route. To him, a happy life with wine, food, and a loving wife is enough. Papageno is not wrong. He is a good man, but what is important to him are the cares and concerns of the personal self. The Prince, on the other hand, is willing to make personal sacrifices to obtain the ultimate prize. He takes the more arduous but more direct route to awakening the inner self, symbolized by finding the beautiful princess.

No matter which path we choose, when we pass through a difficult time, we might remember to dig within ourselves to find the resources, the strength, the hitherto unknown talent buried deep within our own selves, to solve the problem. For it is by solving problems that we develop the inner strength that will enable us to win the final victory.

Chapter Nineteen

THE REWARD PAST ALL TELLING

All valid guideposts point toward the secret gateway. They point, but they themselves cannot lead us to that gateway and the road beyond. Ultimately, it is only our own innermost divine nature that can lead us to the gateway. That divine reality shines through every human being, but in most it shines feebly. That is because our egos are like clouds. Some are dark and threatening. Some are pleasant and fluffy, but each cloud, each ego, blocks the sunlight in varying degrees.

In some individuals, known as adepts, the light shines on the world through a cloudless sky. That light can also influence and guide us, but only if we dissipate the clouds of ego. If we deeply long to alleviate suffering in all its forms, if we are motivated by compassion and altruism, we place ourselves automatically within the stream of influence radiating from the adepts.

At the very heart of the way of life that leads to the secret gateway are two essential requirements: compassion and a relentless pursuit of Truth.

The second of these, a relentless pursuit of Truth, is implied by the Theosophical Society's motto: "There is no religion higher than Truth."

If we persist in holding on to our beliefs in spite of evidence to the contrary, we may fall into a subtle form of selfishness that Blavatsky's teacher Koot Hoomi called a dangerous selfishness "in the higher principles." As an example, he offers the statement that there are persons "so intensely absorbed in the contemplation of their own supposed 'righteousness' that nothing can ever appear right to them outside the focus of their own vision . . . and their judgment of the right and wrong" (*The Mahatma Letters* 441–42).

The adepts reject blind belief, and they encourage us to do the same. Koot Hoomi writes:

> [A student] is at perfect liberty, *and often quite justified from the standpoint of appearances*—to suspect his Guru of being "a fraud" . . . the greater, the sincerer his indignation—whether expressed in words or boiling in his heart—the more fit he is, the better qualified to become an *adept*. He is free to [use] . . . the most abusive words and expressions regarding his guru's actions and orders, provided . . . he resists all and every temptation; rejects every allurement, and proves that nothing, not even the promise of . . . his future adeptship . . . is able to make him deviate from the path of truth and honesty. (*The Mahatma Letters* 222)

A common misconception among some students of the ancient wisdom tradition is the belief that they already have, or must acquire, an *adept* teacher who guides them. Those who believe that they have such a teacher usually think that he guides them psychically. A few believe that they have met their teacher physically. In either case, such people are most likely deluded or in some cases mentally disturbed. That is because, while the adepts claim to influence humanity in the mass, they say that only in extremely rare cases do they take on an individual student. In those cases, the student is nearing the end of the path that leads to adeptship. Those students will have mastered a great deal of what we call paranormal powers, and their lives will be exemplary in every respect. In the passage cited above, Koot Hoomi is referring to such a student.

Nevertheless, it is good advice for anyone on the spiritual path. The prospect of personal reward must never cause us "to deviate from the path of truth and honesty." It should be self-evident that pursuing "the path of truth and honesty" is ultimately best for everyone. Yet few are willing to take a courageous stand that may alienate them from the community. We tend not to want evidence that might contradict our beliefs because a challenge to our worldview threatens our security. Most people prefer the comfort of an acceptable worldview held by many. To allow truth to blot out our personal beliefs requires not only courage, but humility.

In *The Voice of the Silence* we read:

The "Doctrine of the Eye" is for the crowd, the "Doctrine of the Heart," for the elect. The first repeat in pride: "Behold, I know," the last, they who in humbleness have garnered, low confess, "thus have I heard. . . ."

Be humble, if thou wouldst attain to Wisdom. Be humbler still, when Wisdom thou hast mastered. Be like the Ocean which receives all streams and rivers.

The Ocean's mighty calm remains unmoved; it feels them not. (27, 38)

The search for Truth is intricately woven together with compassion. Annie Besant once said that "love is the response that comes from a realization of oneness." Love may be personal or impersonal. Compassion is impersonal love and is a response that comes from a realization of deeper unity. While the search for knowledge alone may lead to selfishness, the search for Truth leads toward realization of unity, and the response to this realization is universal compassion.

Perhaps one of the most powerful statements on compassion ever written is in *The Voice of the Silence*:

Let thy soul lend its ear to every cry of pain like as the lotus bares its heart to drink the morning sun. Let not the fierce sun dry one tear of pain before thyself hast wiped it from the sufferer's eye. But let each burning human tear drop on thy heart and there remain, nor ever brush it off, until the pain that caused it is removed. (12–13)

To "let each burning human tear drop on thy heart" does not mean that we should be in a constant state of depression because of the enormous suffering of others. Compassion is not pity. The latter pulls us down to the level of suffering and makes us suffer along with the sufferer. The former is impersonal in the best sense of the word. It is love of the good and the right that drives us to seek, find, and remove the cause of pain. Individually, we can never remove all pain, but we can dedicate ourselves to discovering and removing the cause of pain wherever we find it. Those who act out of compassion do so joyously. Those who act out of pity may be kind, but they allow themselves to be dragged down to the level of emotional upset. Their own tears then block clear vision, and that renders them helpless.

These two principles, compassion and the relentless pursuit of Truth, are the hallmarks of the true Theosophist. Together they impel us toward the secret gateway, the awakening of the inner self, an altruistic life, and the "regenerating practical Brotherhood" that the adepts say they want. They lead there, that is, if our motive is impersonal and without thought of self.

If in our search we are motivated by hope of personal gain, then we are laying up "treasures upon earth, where moth and rust doth corrupt" (Matt. 6:19). But if we are motivated by what Blavatsky calls "an inexpressible longing for the infinite," we cannot go wrong.

The "moth and rust" that corrupt is a poetic way of saying that everything changes. If we become attached to the pleasures of a changing world, we are bound to suffer when they pass away. Unfortunately there are those who think that the solution to this problem is to become coldly indifferent to the changing world. The true Theosophist will develop a deep appreciation of the changing world, but a calm indifference to the changes.

Since everything changes, then what we believe to be self must also change. If we persist in clinging to the "me" as we know it, we are trying to go against nature. That brings pain. As we identify more and more with the inner self, we find that we appreciate life much more than we did before. We do not love friends and family less. We love them more because we realize a deeper unity with them. We even appreciate the personalities of loved ones more because we accept the natural flow of change. Those who see the enduring reality behind the changes and identify with that are the true Theosophists, whether they are members of the Society or not.

Theosophy always points toward the eternal reality beyond the sensate world. It is ultimately an optimistic philosophy because it assures us that we can realize our unity with the Eternal. The fruits of a Theosophical life are ever-increasing inner peace and outer joy. Theosophy will not free us from growth pains, but it will help us to understand them and to realize that by passing through them we come closer to freedom from all pain.

Living a Theosophical life with all our heart is not easy, but was there ever anything worthwhile that was easy? Great athletes, dancers, and musicians must work hard to achieve expertise. Once it is achieved, they are free to enjoy the fruit of their labor. With effort, we can discover the immortal self and experience the inexpressible joy that results from that discovery. Those who follow the light of Theosophy will find that each small victory along the way brings its own reward. They get more pleasure out of life, not less. Yet, driven by compassion and a quest for Truth, they never take their eyes off of the final goal of union with the infinite.

On the road to the final goal we must gradually develop an iron determination, and yet be gentle and humble. We must be clad with the armor of courage, take up the shield of purity, and wield the sword of intellect. If we continue to try in spite of our many failures, we will eventually discover the secret gateway. Following the steep and thorny road that leads beyond, we may come at last to self-knowledge. Only then will we be free. Only then will we reap the final reward past all telling, the power to bless and save humanity.

References

Augustine. *Exposition on the Psalms.* Quoted on service leaflet, Church of St. Mary the Virgin, New York, NY.

Ballou, Robert, Friedrich Spiegelberg, and Horace L. Friess, eds. *The Bible of the World.* New York: Viking, 1939.

Besant, Annie. *Dharma.* Adyar, Madras, India: Theosophical Publishing House, 1981.

———. *The Spiritual Life,* Wheaton, IL: Theosophical Publishing House, Quest Books, 1991.

Blavatsky, Helena Petrovna. *The Collected Writings.* 15 vols. Wheaton, IL: Theosophical Publishing House, 1966–91.

———. *The Voice of the Silence.* Wheaton, IL: Theosophical Publishing House, Quest Books, 1992.

———. *The Secret Doctrine.* 3 vols. Wheaton, IL: Theosophical Publishing House, Quest Books, 1993.

Diamond, Jared. *Collapse: How Societies Choose to Fail or Succeed.* New York: Viking, 2004.

Fagg, Lawrence W. *Two Faces of Time.* Wheaton, IL: Theosophical Publishing House, Quest Books, 1985.

Jinarajadasa, C., ed. *Letters from the Masters of the Wisdom, First Series,* Adyar, Madras, India: Theosophical Publishing House, 1964.

————, ed. *Letters from the Masters of the Wisdom, Second Series.* Adyar, Madras, India: Theosophical Publishing House, 1973.

Kunz, Dora. *The Personal Aura.* Wheaton, IL: Theosophical Publishing House, Quest Books, 1991.

The Liturgy of the Liberal Catholic Church. London: St. Alban Press, 1983.

The Mahatma Letters to A. P. Sinnett. In Chronological Sequence. Comp. A. T. Barker. Ed. Vicente Hao Chin, Jr. Quezon City, Manila, Philippines: Theosophical Publishing House, 1993.

Nicholson, Shirley J. *Ancient Wisdom — Modern Insight.* Wheaton, IL: Theosophical Publishing House, Quest Books, 1985.

Plotinus. *The Enneads.* Translated by Stephen MacKenna. Burdett, NY: Larson, 1992.

Waterman, Adlai E. *Obituary: The "Hodgson Report" on Madame Blavatsky.* Adyar, Madras, India: Theosophical Publishing House, 1963.

Whitman, Walt. *Leaves of Grass.* New York: Viking, 1959.

Suggested Readings

Algeo, John. *Getting Acquainted with The Secret Doctrine: A Study Course.* Revised edition. Wheaton, IL: Department of Education, Theosophical Society in America, 1990.

Besant, Annie. *Dharma.* Adyar, Madras, India: Theosophical Publishing House, 1981.

———. *The Spiritual Life,* Wheaton, IL: Theosophical Publishing House, Quest Books, 1991.

Blavatsky, Helena Petrovna. *The Collected Writings.* 15 vols. Edited by Boris de Zirkoff. Wheaton IL: Theosophical Publishing House, 1966–91.

> The most complete and definitive collection of Blavatsky's articles and miscellaneous writings, arranged in chronological order covering the years 1874–91. Volume 15 is a cumulative index.

———. *The Inner Group Teachings of H. P. Blavatsky to Her Personal Pupils, 1890–91.* Edited by H. J. Spierenburg. 2nd ed. San Diego, CA: Point Loma Publications, 1995.

———. *Isis Unveiled: A Master-Key to the Mysteries of Ancient and Modern Science and Theology.* Edited by Boris de Zirkoff. Wheaton, IL: Theosophical Publishing House, 1972. Originally published 1877.

———. *The Key to Theosophy: An Abridgement.* Edited by Joy Mills. Wheaton, IL: Theosophical Publishing House, Quest Books, 1981.

———. *The Secret Doctrine: The Synthesis of Science, Religion and Philosophy.* 3 vols. Edited by Boris de Zirkoff. Wheaton, IL: Theosophical Publishing House, Quest Books, 1993.

———. *The Voice of the Silence: Being Chosen Fragments from the "Book of the Golden Precepts" for Daily Use of Lanoos (Disciples).* Wheaton, IL: Theosophical Publishing House, Quest Books, 1992.

Caldwell, Daniel. *The Esoteric World of Madame Blavatsky: Insights into the Life of a Modern Sphinx.* Wheaton, IL: Theosophical Publishing House, Quest Books, 2000.

Collins, Mabel. *Light on the Path.* Wheaton, IL: Theosophical Publishing House, 1980.

Cranston, Sylvia. *H.P.B.: The Extraordinary Life and Influence of Helena Blavatsky, Founder of the Modern Theosophical Movement.* 3rd ed. Santa Barbara, CA: Path Publishing House, 1998.

Hanson, Virginia. *An Introduction to The Mahatma Letters: A Study Course.* Wheaton, IL: Department of Education, Theosophical Society in America, 1996.

Harrison, Vernon. *H. P. Blavatsky and the SPR: An Examination of the Hodgson Report of 1885.* Pasadena, CA: Theosophical University Press, 1997.

Huxley, Aldous. *The Perennial Philosophy.* New York: Harper & Row, 1970.

Jinarajadasa, C., ed. *Letters from the Masters of the Wisdom, First and Second Series.* Adyar, Madras, India: Theosophical Publishing House, 1964, 1973.

Krishnamurti, J. (Alcyone) *At the Feet of the Master.* Wheaton, IL: Theosophical Publishing House, 1974. Originally published 1910.

Kunz, Dora. *The Personal Aura.* Wheaton, IL: Theosophical Publishing House, Quest Books, 1991.

The Mahatma Letters to A. P. Sinnett. In Chronological Sequence. Compiled by A. T. Barker. Edited by Vicente Hao Chin, Jr. Quezon City, Manila, Philippines: Theosophical Publishing House, 1993.

Nicholson, Shirley J. *Ancient Wisdom — Modern Insight.* Wheaton, IL: Theosophical Publishing House, Quest Books, 1985.

Prem, Sri Krishna, and Sri Madhava Ashish. *Man, the Measure of All Things.* Wheaton, IL: Theosophical Pubishing House, 1969.

Stevenson, Ian. *European Cases of the Reincarnation Type.* Jefferson, NC: McFarland & Co., 2003.

Waterman, Adlai E. *Obituary: The "Hodgson Report" on Madame Blavatsky.* Adyar, Madras, India: Theosophical Publishing House, 1963.

INDEX

Index

Index

INDEX

INDEX

INDEX

Quest Books

encourages open-minded inquiry into
world religions, philosophy, science, and the arts
in order to understand the wisdom of the ages,
respect the unity of all life, and help people explore
individual spiritual self-transformation.

Its publications are generously supported by
The Kern Foundation,
a trust committed to Theosophical education.

Quest Books is the imprint of
the Theosophical Publishing House,
a division of the Theosophical Society in America.
For information about programs, literature,
on-line study, membership benefits, and international centers,
see www.theosophical.org
or call 800-669-1571 or (outside the U.S.) 630-668-1571.

Related Quest Titles

Foundations of the Ageless Wisdom, Edward Abdill
(DVD or video, also study guide)

The Pilgrim Self, Robert Ellwood

The Power of Thought, John Algeo and Shirley J. Nicholson

The Seven Human Powers, Shirley J. Nicholson

To order books or a complete Quest catalog,
call 800-669-9425 or (outside the U.S.) 630-665-0130.